APHRODITE C1
Goddess of Love

THE MYTHOLOGY OF CYPRUS

Stass Paraskos

Foreword by
George Thomas — Viscount Tonypandy

Editor
Dr. S. Panteli

INTERWORLD PUBLICATIONS

LONDON.

First Published 1988 in Great Britain
by Interworld Publications
12 The Fairway, New Barnet,
Herts. EN5 1HN
Tel: 01-449 5938

First published 1988 in Cyprus
by Interworld Publications

ISBN: 0 948853 05 0

Typeset in 11 point Plantin 2 point leaded
by Sunset Typesetters, London N9
Design and Planning by Tophill Designs, New Barnet, Herts.
Printed and binded in Cyprus by PRINTCO LTD.
Cover: Photograph by R.G. Lavithis showing the birthplace of Aphrodite
        — Paphos, Cyprus
Illustration of Aphrodite based on Bodichelli by Eddie Brockwell

CONTENTS

CHAPTER THREE
**THE TRAVELS OF
BRONTEAS**

CHAPTER FOUR
**SURVIVING INFLUENCES
OF THE CULT OF
APHRODITE

APPENDIX
Cyprus Through the

EDITOR'S INTRODUCTION

Aphrodite, one of the ancient world's most beautiful women, has long been a figure of mystery and legend. Stass Paraskos tears away the shrouds that have hidden antiquitie's *Goddess of Love* and reveals a life rich in excitement, intrigue and tragedy.

To open this book is to enter into the extraordinary world of one of mythology's most intriguing people, Aphrodite: Goddess, Mother, Lover — a fascinating woman.

The Book falls into four main sectors; each one with its own individuality and each one with its many descriptive passages.

Chapter One – **"Aphrodite Cypris"**, brings to us a fascinating insight into the mysteries of Aphrodite's birth, lovers, children and life. Of special interest is her role during the Trojan War and the subsequent Fall of Troy.

Chapter Two – **"The Cinyraid Circle"**, brings us into touch with characters such as Pygmalion, Adonis, and the rites of paganism, sacrifice and divination which were widely practised in Cyprus before the advent of Christianity.

Chapter Three – **"The Travels of Bronteas"**, takes us to the main cities of Cyprus and discusses the customs, life and characteristics which prevailed in them. Certainly a unique chapter of great imaginative scholarship.

Chapter Four – **"Surviving Influences of the Cult of Aphrodite in Cyprus"**, is delightful and concise. Cyprus' mythological and legendary past is transformed into the realities of religious life and practice in the 20th century.

The reader can now judge for himself — herself!

Dr. S. Panteli
1.1.1988

THE AUTHOR

The author **Stass Paraskos** is one of Cyprus' leading painters and the head of the summer school there. Currently he is a senior lecturer in Painting at Canterbury College of Art, England

He has exhibited widely in Cyprus, in the United Kingdom and in other European countries and the United States.

His other publications include 'Cyprus of Copper' 1969 and 'Cyprus Myths and Legends' 1978. He has also published numerous articles on Art in newspapers and magazines.

Stass Paraskos in his Cyprus Studio.

ACKNOWLEGEMENTS

There are so many people whom I have to thank for their help, contributions and advice that I fear that some may be omitted, and to these I make my apologies.

First, I would like to thank Viscount Tonypandy (George Thomas, ex-Speaker of the House of Commons), for his masterly foreword. Next, I must thank George Szirtes who edited the third chapter, 'The Travels of Bronteas'.

Thirdly, I am forever grateful to Dr. S. Panteli for his valuable advice, brief introduction and editing of the whole book. My thanks also to Renos and Anna Lavithis who both read the typescript and made some constructive suggestions.

I sincerely thank my Publishers for the trust they had placed on me to rewrite and enlarge my book on the "Mythology of Cyprus", and for their efficiency and speed in bringing out this 'new' study.

I am forever grateful to my wife Winifred Mary who did all the typing.

Finally, I wish to reiterate that the shortcomings of the book remain entirely my own.

FOREWORD

Greek mythology provides an eternal fascination.

The sheer beauty, grace and dignity with which the stories of the gods are decorated stirs the imagination of each successive generation.

Stass Paraskos, one of Cyprus' most distinguished artists, provides in this book an exciting recital of the influence Greek mythology has brought to bear on Greek Cypriot development.

The detailed research which underlies this book is evident in every page.

Those who love Cyprus will find this account exhilarating beyond measure. It adds distinction to the already rich store of books about one of the loveliest island countries in all the world. Schools and libraries cannot afford to be without it.

Because my love of Cyprus is deep and strong, I shall cherish this book.

George Thomas–Viscount Tonypandy.

The Birth of Venus, by Sandro Botticelli.

Venus – by Tiziano, Uffizi Gallery – Florence.

Chapter One

APHRODITE CYPRIS

THE BIRTH OF APHRODITE

The Worship of Aphrodite was as widely diffused around the Mediterranean lands as that of any other Hellenic Divinity. We find it in the country of Attica, in the city and the coast; in Megara, Corinth, and the Corinthian colonies; in Sicyon, Hermione, Epidaurus, and Argos; in Laconia there was a special and important form of worship; there are comparatively slight traces of it in Arcadia, but abundant testimony of its prevalence in Elis and on the coast of Achaea. However the most famous centres of the cult were the Greek islands (the three "Cs") **Cyprus, Crete, and Cythera.**

That such discrepancies should occur, is due chiefly to the prevailing attitude of the period. In Cyprus for instance where the Greek element in the population had been dominant from an early stage, a very liberal manner was quite common, whereby people could speak as they liked about the deities. Even theocratic cities like Paphos were influenced by this attitude which allowed men to indulge in battles of wits against their gods, believing that it was possible to gain their favours by promises, bribery or flattery. Each man was free to interpret matters in his own way — there was very little of the religious dogma as we understand it. Instead of an official religion they had their myths and legends, some created by poets others invented by popular imagination, and through these they tried to understand the world and explain its mysteries. The nearest equivalent to a sacred text was poetry wherein they could find diverse views and accounts of the key legends. Thus it was quite possible for various communities to select poems or passages which they could further their claim to be the home of the goddess. This also explains the contradictions we find in Aphrodite's character throughout classicial literature. Some people believed that she was the daughter of Zeus and others that she was his mistress but this does not mean, as some writers have claimed, that she was both the daughter and mistress of Zeus.

Hesiod describes her birth in the following fashion.

He tells how, by the agency of **Gaes,** her son **Cronos** the Titan escaped the fate of his brothers and sisters, who, as soon as they were born were confined to the infernal regions by their father **Uranus,** the ruler of the skies, and how, when Cronos grew up, he witnessed his mother and father making love among the planets, whereupon he mutilated the evil Uranus, castrating him so that his genitals fell into the sea.

The severed organs floated for a long time in the ocean and a white foam gathered round them, which was fertilized by the sperm. Out of this strange froth sprang a beautiful goddess. At first the winds carried her towards Cythera but then Zephyrus, the west wind, took command and guided her to the Cyprian coast, to the site of **Paphos,** where she was welcomed by the *Seasons* and by *Eros,* the winged god of love, who was to be her constant companion.

Wherever her feet touched the ground there blossomed all manner of flowering plants. The *Graces* then dressed her in the kind of attire that they themselves assumed when attending the dances of the immortals, decking her in luxurious gowns and jewels including a magic girdle — the famous *"kestos imas"*, and setting a crown of gold upon her head. Accompanied by Eros and *Pothos,* the god of longing, she journeyed thence to Olympus in order to claim her place among the assembly of gods. Here she was named **Aphrodite** because she was born of the sea-foam, and **Cypris** as Cyprus was the land where she first appeared. Her great beauty aroused the envy of the goddesses, but the gods greeted her with enthusiasm and many tried to gain her affection.

Zeus, the father of gods, allocated her a very wide realm. She was to be the goddess of beauty, of joy and laughter; the Queen of all aspects of love, the guardian of young girls, and governess of the fertility of animals and plants, (to this end a number of prolific creatures were to be her sacred symbols including the goat, the rabbit, the sparrow, and the apple tree whose consecrated fruit used to be given by priests to women who wished to become pregnant).

Her powers over women was so overwhelming that some of them were led to disaster against their will, as was the case of Helen who was made to betray her husband and abandon her country to follow Paris to Troy thus causing the ten year Trojan war. Similarly Pasiphae, Medea and Phaidra

Above Top: Shell-birth   Aphrodite with roses and winged Erotes–c.5th cent. BC.
Above: Aphrodite is raised from the sea by two nymphs – Villa Ludovisi, Italy.
Left: Venus Anadyomene (birth of Venus)

fell victims of Aphrodite and were destroyed by their mad passion for the wrong men. In addition to these powers Aphrodite was to be the protectress of women in dangerous vocations such as prostitutes who were allowed to exercise their profession in some of her temples; and to be the guardian of marriage in which office she was offered sacrifices at wedding ceremonies. Widows and spinsters prayed to her for a partner.

Aphrodite's favourite birds were the doves, which accompanied her on some of her journeys, and the swans which drove her chariot across the skies. Her favourite plant was the aromatic Myrtle and her favourite flower the pink rose. Everything about Aphrodite was beautiful and poetic. Inevitably she became a very popular goddess and her cult spread to all the Mediterranean countries resulting in the multifarious nature of the Aphrodite we know.

Her surname varied according to the place of worship; thus at Paphos she was known as **Aphrodite Paphia** but other cities referred to her by their own respective titles, of *Amathusia, Cythera, Exopolis, Collias* etc. Besides her toponimic titles, there were also surnames that were derived from the natures of various cults. For instance in some places she was called *Epistrophia* because of her association with incestuous enjoyment; elsewhere she was known as *Philomeda* for her love of the phallus, *Philomeis* for her love of laughter, *Hetera* for her patronage of prostitutes, *Apaturia* because she deceived in love, *Verticordia* because she made women cultivate chastity, and *Calipyge* because of her beautiful backside and her love of transvestites. There was even a male Aphrodite in Cyprus whose statue had a beard and male genitals and was probably called *Aphroditus*. At Orlomenus there was a temple of *Aphrodite Argynnis* which comes from the name of a youth with very white skin for whom Agamemnon saw bathing, and felt a passion. In his effort to avoid the advances of the great king the youth drowned in the river. Agamemnon buried the body and built a temple in his memory which he dedicated to Aphrodite Argynnis.

At the Greek town of Trikke they worshipped *"Aphrodite the Mankiller"* a name relating to the murder of the famous prostitute Lais in the temple of Aphrodite by the women of the city and the revenge Aphrodite took against the murderers by killing their menfolk. At Thebes she was worshipped under three separate names. It is not surprising therefore that Aphrodite has been thought to be the common name for several goddesses, for even her lineage was disputed some believing her to be the daughter of Uranus, while others affirmed that Zeus and Dione were her parents. Nevertheless, it has not been explained why Dione rather than Hera was selected as her adopted mother.

Aphrodite's most common surnames were **Urania** (which means heavenly) and *Pandemos* (universal). Many people believed that under the first she was the goddess of spiritual love and under the second of sexual pleasures but this is dubious for some temples, such as those of Corinth and Paphos, while being dedicated to Aphrodite Urania were in fact notorious centres of sexual activity. It seems that the epithet Pandemos was first used in Athens when king Theseus built a temple to Aphrodite for the worship *"of all people"* (Pandemos) of the city and not just for one district (the city was divided into municipal areas). That many people believed her to be promiscuous is due to some extent to her connection with fertility, but to give some example of the contradictory nature of legends surrounding her, the following story tells of her as the protectress of young virgins.

Pandareus had stolen the golden dog that watched over the temple of Zeus in Crete. He gave it to *Tantalus,* the king of Lydia, who when confronted by *Hermes,* denied possession of the article and thus incurred the wrath of the gods. Hermes, who was not deceived by the king's talk, seized the golden dog by force and dumped Mount Sipylus on top of the impious monarch. The thief Pandareus, who had fled to Sicily, perished soon afterwards along with his wife leaving two young daughters called *Merope* and *Cleodora,* who would not have survived for long, had not Aphrodite taken them into her care. She fed them with milk and honey and wine, and cultivated their exceptional beauty, persuading other goddesses to be liberal with their gifts, so that wisdom, joy and skill made them into models of ideal womenhood. When the girls matured, Aphrodite went to Olympus, to request from Zeus kind and tender husbands for them, but in her absence the cruel *Harpies* carried off the virgins and gave them as slaves to the *Erinyes,* the avenging deities, as punishment for their father's crime.

This story illustrates Aphrodite's love of innocence and there were many cases where in spite of the generally held opinion that her temples were centres of licentiousness, strict rules of chastity were imposed on the priestesses. In the temple of *Aphrodite Akrea* in Cyprus, for instance, where Aphrodite was represented holding a rose in one hand and a pomegranate in the other, only virgins were accepted for the priesthood.

In her temple at Sykion, where an ivory statue by Kanachus represented the goddess in a sitting position, only priestesses who had sworn to remain virgins for ever were allowed into the sacred enclosure, and in Sparta they had two statues of Aphrodite in the same temple, one showing her fully armed, as the defender of the virtues of womanhood, and the other showing her bound in chains to symbolise the bond between wives and husbands.

Aphrodite's more scandalous reputation was got chiefly in times of moral decadence, like the Hellenistic period when the Ptolemaic queens of Egypt and Cyprus claimed to personify the goddess in her role as the queen of love and their courts built altars and temples to them, and the nobles organised orgiastic feasts for their mistresses, all of whom were named after Aphrodite and claimed to be in honour of the goddess.

Intellectual Athens of the classicial and Hellenistic periods also contributed to Aphrodite's promiscuous reputation. Great and influential artists like Praxiteles and Apelles used common prostitutes like Phryne and Lais as models for paintings and sculptures representing the Goddess and became fashionable for Athenian men to associate with prostitutes. At the same time, many students of the philosopher Epicurus came to the conclusion that the only purpose in life was to seek pleasure.

As a result of these attitudes, public morals changed and so did the character of the goddess of love. Aphrodite became the favourite goddess of prostitutes who celebrated her festivals with orgies and used their fortunes to build monuments and temples in which Aphrodite was represented as a harlot.

We have seen how Aphrodite meted out harsh punishment on mortals who had offended her but some myths show the goddess in a benevolent light towards men and women. One beneficiary was the shepherd Selemnus who was abandoned by the nymph *Argyra* because he grew old. Aphrodite transformed him into a river first but his gloom continued even after his transformation and then the goddess helped him a second time by making him forget his sadness. From then on all who bathed in the waters of Selemnus river were cured of any sadness caused by unhappy love.

The merchant Dexicreon from Samos also benefited from Aphrodite's benevolence. As he was about to load his ship with all kinds of goods Aphrodite advised him to abandon his plans, and to load up instead with fresh water and sail away at once. Some distance from the coast the winds stopped blowing and many ships were unable to sail to their destinations. Soon they ran out of drinking water and Dexicreon sold his cargo to make a fortune. When he returned to his native Samos he commissioned a statue of the goddess which was much admired in ancient times.

APHRODITE'S HUSBAND

Although Aphrodite was the guardian of married life, she herself was not a faithful wife. This may have been due to her misfortune in being paired with **Hephaistus,** a match to which she did not willingly assent to but appearances apart, her husband was not a dull character. He was the god of fire and the patron of all those who worked in metal; he was the greatest of all craftsmen and came of the highest stock being the child of Zeus and Hera.

Zeus himself gave away the bride and received from Hephaistus a bowl of excellent workmanship. To Aphrodite he offered as his first gift a necklace sparkling with precious stones. The poet Apollonios spoke of Hephaistus giving his bride a palace as a wedding gift and Cladianus (another poet) wrote that she received from him a piece of land surrounded by a golden fence, containing palaces of gold and precious stones. This was situated on a mountain of Cyprus, inaccessible to mortals, where a sweet climate prevailed, where the soil produces without being cultivated and where there are two springs among green foliage. There lived Aphrodite surrounded by Erotes: a kind of paradise which has been identified with the site known as the **'Baths of Aphrodite'.**

Left: "Baths of Aphrodite" near Polis-Paphos. Right: Hephaestus.

17

At Hephaistus' birth he was found to be lame and so ugly that his mother, disgusted, cast him from the heights of Mount Olympus into the ocean in the hope that he would be drowned. However he was fated to be saved by the sea-nymphs *Thetis* and *Eurynome* who carried him to the ocean bed where they looked after him for nine years.

He was so grateful for their kindness that he made for them several artifices in metal. Finding that he had an aptitude for this he practised assiduously until he became a supreme craftsman, so skilled that he was able to make two ingenious statues that were able to walk and act as his assistants.

Hephaistus then set about seeking revenge on his mother. He constructed a splendid throne of gold fitted with secret chains and sent it to Hera, who was so thrilled with it that she immediately sat down, touching off the cunning mechanism. At once the chains held her fast and she was powerless to remove them. Neither were the other gods any more successful and Hera besides being uncomfortable, felt extremely humiliated. When it was realised that Hephaistus was the only god with the ability to release her, the gods sent messengers down to the ocean to plead for his assistance, but they met with a blank refusal. Threats and entreaties were of no avail until **Dionysus,** the God of Wine, tricked him into sampling some of his most potent wines, and dumping the intoxicated Smith-god on the back of a mule, transported him to the top of Mount Olympus. Even in his drunken state however Hephaistus refused to free his mother and would only relent when finally the gods promised him the pick of the goddesses for his wife. Being an artist, with a love of beauty he naturally chose the most beautiful of them all, Aphrodite, and thus it was that this most unlikely match was made.

Hephaistus later forgave his mother and thenceforth treated her with respect and on one occasion went so far as to take her part in an argument she had with Zeus. The king of Gods was so enraged by this that in a fit of fury he seized his son by the leg and threw him down from Mount Olympus. This great fall lasted for nine days from top till bottom and that would have been the end of Hephaistus had not the inhabitants of Lemnos caught him just before he reached the ground. The god was grateful to the people of Lemnos and grew so fond of them that he decided to make his home on their island. In his forge he had the assistance of the one-eyed giants named **Cyclopes** who helped him to make all those wonders of art and craftsmanship for which he was famous. His achievements included the construction of the thunder bolts of Zeus, the armour of gods and heroes, the fire-breathing bulls of the king of Colchis and all the palaces of the immortals. His own palace on Olympus was imperishable and as bright as the stars; it contained his own workshop with the anvil and twenty bellows. In spite of his skill and labour, Hephaistus was constantly ridiculed by the other gods for his ugliness. Homer describes how this kindliest of gods was mocked as he hobbled round, serving the other gods at banquets on Olympus. Even Aphrodite, his wife mimicked his lameless when she wanted to amuse her lovers.

But Hephaistus was no more faithful to Aphrodite than she was to him, numbering among his mistresses the graces *Charis* and *Aglaia* who acted as handmaids to his wife and were responsible for Refinement and Gentleness. None of Aphrodite's children were fathered by him but he had several illegitimate children of his own and he treated them all, both Aphrodite's, and his own, with kindness and consideration.

On one occasion he managed to turn the tables on his flighty wife and her current lover **Ares,** the god of War. Ares was one of the twelve Olympians and as such was honoured by the people of Cyprus, though it must be said that this was due more to fear than affection for he was known to be bad-tempered and on occasion extremely brutal. Being the son of Zeus and Hera he naturally inherited their qualities of courage and leadership but Zeus often had to reprimand him for his hot-blooded excesses, which annoyed the other gods. Besides he was impulsive and lack of thought sometimes led to his downfall as when he was defeated and bound by Poseidon's two gigantic sons, *Oeus* and *Ephialtes.* This cost him thirteen months of liberty. Another time he challenged Hercules to single combat, in order to avenge the death of his son *Cycnus,* but was wounded and forced to flee, groaning, to Olympus. Indeed this incident might have cost him dearer had not Zeus intervened in the first place to save him from further punishment. During the Trojan war he tried to play off both ends against the middle by sometimes supporting the Greeks and sometimes the Trojans so that the war was prolonged for ten years. But he did not escape scot free for when a battle was in progress he ventured to attack **Athena** who knocked him down with a stone. Further evidence of his vindictive nature may be found in the following story:

Ares had been secretly meeting Aphrodite for some time believing that the arrangements were fool-proof but one day as the sun was passing the windows of Hephaistus's palace he saw them entwined on the bed. Hephaistus was at work at the time but the sun, as soon as his course had taken him to a position above the forge, told the smith-god of what he had seen. Hephaistus let out a deep earth shaking moan and wept. In a jealous rage he plotted his revenge. He used all his skill to make from fire and steel a net so strong that it could not be broken, but at the same time so fine that not even a god could see it. When he returned that night he set this net above Aphrodite's bed so that the slightest movement would cause it to drop. Then he announced his intention of paying a visit to the people of Lemnos. The next morning he set off.

On hearing this Ares was overjoyed and threw caution to the winds. He sped to the palace were he met the waiting Aphrodite and straight away they tumbled onto the bed in a passionate embrace. At this point the net fell on top of them and they were trapped.

Again it was the sun who performed the messenger's role and Hephaistus soon learned of the success of his scheme. He returned home as quickly as he could to find the lovers locked together in the very position that they had first assumed before the net had fallen. The sight of his unfaithful wife arrested in the act of love stung him deeply and in a mixture of exasperation and triumph he uttered a terrible cry which roused the other gods and brought them running to the scene. A delicate situation awaited them and the goddesses blushed and returned to their homes but the gods remained in the hall, nudging each other and laughing heartily at what they saw. Some professed to be outraged but could scarcely suppress a giggle, some exchanged well worn truisms applicable to the situation, while **Hermes** who himself was in love with Aphrodite declared that even if the chains were twice as constricting he would gladly change places with Ares. The other gods continued guying the lovers and some remembered how in such situations it was customary to extract a fine from the adulterous couple.

In the uproar only **Poseidon** was concerned for the lover's dignity and he urged Hephaistus to let them go, offering to ensure that Ares would pay the adultery fine. But Hephaistus would have none of it and replied that it was manifestly wrong to stand bail for scoundrels who would seize the next opportunity to escape from their obligations. Only when Poseidon offered to pay the money himself did the cuckolded Hephaistus relent and loosen the net.

The embarrassed lovers got to their feet and departed rather ungracefully for their limbs were stiff and their muscles cramped from their long entrapment. Ashamed Ares went off to nurse his wounded pride in Thrace while Aphrodite returned to her birthplace in Paphos where the three *Graces* bathed her and anointed her with oils and a rare perfume the aroma of which, it was said, never fades. They robed her in rich gowns and soon she was restored to all her radiance and beauty, not yet aware that she was carrying the child who was to be called **Harmonia.**

But Aphrodite did not forgive the busybody sun who betrayed her to Hephaistus. She avenged herself by inspiring in him a burning passion for *Leucothea*, daughter of the king of Babylon. In order to introduce himself to Leucothea he took on the appearance of her mother and visited her but Leucothea's jealous sister, who also loved the sun, discovered what was going on and betrayed them to her father. The king was furious and ordered his own daughter to be buried alive. The Sun, unable to save his beloved from death, sprinkled nectar and ambrosia on the tomb and the body of Leucothea was turned into an aromatic shrub.

After the incident which made him the laughing stock of Olympus, Ares transferred his affection to *Eos*, the 'rosy-fingered dawn'. Aphrodite grew jealous and tempted Eos to numerous love affairs with mortals the last of these being *Tithonus*, a prince of Troy, by whom she had two sons. Wishing to be bound to her new lover for eternity Eos begged Zeus to make him immortal, but unfortunately she had forgotten to ask for perpetual youth and beauty and soon he grew into a decrepit old man. Eventually he was reduced to a wrinkled mass of flesh, unable to enjoy life in any way and begged the gods to remove him from this world. But he was immortal and his request could not be granted so the gods changed him into a grasshopper instead.

Top: Aphrodite and Ares trapped in bed by her husband Hephaestus. Other gods look on laughing.
Left: The Sun (Helios).
Far Left: Hera, the Farnese.

21

THE CHILDREN OF APHRODITE

At this point we should mention the children born to Aphrodite by her several lovers, for we have seen she was not a faithful wife. The child fathered by *Dionysus* was probably the most notable of these. He was named **Priapus** and came to occupy quite an important place among the minor gods, indeed in some parts of Italy and Greece, he was worshipped in the same temple as were his mother and father. In Asia Minor he claimed the status of a major god for there he had his own temples and festivals. It is well known that Priapus was of a some-what peculiar appearance, and the cause of his disfigurement is worth recounting.

Relations between Aphrodite and Zeus' wife, *Hera,* had never been too happy, for Hera had felt right from the beginning that the young goddess had upstaged her with her beauty.

Besides, Hera had born Hephaistus, a son both lame and ugly and she could well imagine how comely a child of Aphrodite's might be. So she spitefully decided to interfere with the natural process of birth in order to forestall further shame. Feigning friendship with the goddess she offered to assist her at the child's delivery but her objective was to exercise some power over the new being. Through her interference the child was born deformed in all his parts; he had a human enough face, but the overall shape of his head was that of a phallus and his ears were goatlike. He was in fact the visual epitomy of lust, a subtle caricature of his mother's propensities. Aphrodite was disgusted and so ashamed of his ugliness that she straightaway exposed him on a mountain in the hope that he would die. But, as often happens with things that we wish to lose or destroy, the despised Priapus was found by some shepherds from Lampascus and saved from his intended doom. The appearance of the child was deemed a marvel in the local villages and soon he became the favourite god of the district. Later however they discovered the correspondence between his features and his nature and were forced to expel him owing to the frequency with which he was seducing their wives. As it happened the town was smitten soon after by a terrible disease whose cause they attributed to their dismissal of the strange little god, and so Priapus was reinstated and a great temple was built in his honour which was to become notorious for the riotous debauchery that took place within. Roman brides in later times were required to sit astride in image of Priapus and at Greek marriages an effigy in the shape of the phallus god was carried in procession in a basket. Red priapic amulets were exhibited near prized possessions and were worn by people round their necks for protection against the evil eye. This was because the ancients believe that the god's obscene shape attracted the first and most dangerous glance of a malevolent being. Thus it was a standard practice to place such images in prominent positions near private dwellings and many household goods were given phallic form. In Roman times a stone pillar with a bearded head and erect penis stood outside most public buildings. The customary sacrifice offered to Priapus was an ass because this animal by its braying had woken the nymph Lotis when the god was about to rape her.

Another son of Aphrodite, although the product of a purely divine union attained rather less prominence. *Hermes* was his father and he was appropriately called **Hermaphroditus.** Though he was an extremely handsome youth he proved to be of an androgynous nature. But this was not so from the beginning. Ovid tells the story of his transformations. He relates how at the age of fifteen the boy set out on a long journey in order to acquire knowledge, to encounter and overcome hardship and thus to gain respect and attain manhood. On his way he passed by a fountain of the water-nymph *Samalcis* who had scorned hunting and all the common pursuits of other nymphs, and who had somehow managed to avoid the notice of *Diana the Great Huntress*. She was extremely strong willed and rather vain, and when she saw the handsome youth she was determined to make him her own. At first she tried to gain his affection by direct physical advances, but the boy was innocent and merely confused by her behaviour. So she pretended to go away but instead hid herself behind a tree. It being a hot day the boy was tired and thirsty and the cool waters of the fountain were a great temptation. Thinking that he was in absolute privacy he took off his clothes and entered the water, whereupon Samalcis, grateful for this opportunity emerged from her hiding place and was quickly beside him. She attempted by quick movements to twine herself around him but this was not easy as he struggled against her and kept slipping out of her clutches; they fought a long time, rising and falling from the water but his strength was greater than hers and eventually she began to weaken. Realising that she might lose him she prayed to the gods that they should not be separated, and thus it was that their bodies were there and then joined together and it became impossible to tell whether the new creature was male or female or both. Thenceforth all men tho bathed in the fountain of Samalcis became effeminate.

Hermaphroditus was a popular god in many lands where his fun-loving worshippers used to organise colourful festivals at which men dressed as women and women as men.

There were two other children of Aphrodite sired by gods. *Eryx* fathered by Poseidon, and *Harmonia* who had Ares for a father.

Eryx is chiefly known for his foolish challenge to Hercules to a trial of strength, this not surprisingly resulted in his death. He was buried on a mountain in Sicily which thenceforth bore his name. On Mount Eryx was also buried Aphrodite's lover *Anchises* and on its summit the goddess had one of her most celebrated temples inside which a fire was burning continuously without leaving any ash.

Harmonia was especially honoured by the people of Boeotia who believed that her father Ares was Aphrodite's legitimate husband, and not her lover.

The aristocracy of Boeotia claimed descent from Harmonia like Roman aristocracy in later years claimed descent from Aphrodite's son **Aeneas.** Harmonia grew up to marry Cadmus, king of Thebes. Everyone attended the marriage ceremony, except Hera whose grudge against Aphrodite now extended to her children. Of course there were magnificent presents from all the guests but none more beautiful than the necklace given by *Cadmus* himself to his bride. It had been made by Hephaistus whose skill in such craft was legendary, and it glittered and sparkled as the light danced on it. Wearing it Harmonia looked more captivating than ever.

The royal couple lived happily together for some years while Harmonia bore the king five children, a son and four daughters. But it was on these children that Hera vent her spite and tragedy and humiliation befell every one of them in turn until the load of grief grew too heavy for the royal couple to bear and they in their old age abandoned themselves to self-exile in Illyria; but this only intensified their sorrow and at last they begged Zeus to relieve them of their misery. He heard and acted promptly on their behalf. Cadmus and Harmonia were transformed into serpents winding and coiling around each other. So that they should be happier in their strange new life, Zeus led them into the blessed fields of Elysium, the resting place for virtuous heroes.

As for the spendid necklace, it passed through several hands from that time on, but it had acquired an aura of evil, a malevolent influence that proved fatal to those who possessed it, including among others the Argonaut *Amphiarus,* his son *Alcmaeon* and the *king of Phegeus.* It is said that the last owner of the necklace offered it in sacrifice in the temple of Adonis and Aphrodite at Amathus in Cyprus where it adorned the neck of one of the goddess' statues.

Aphrodite's children, included **Aeneas,** the hero of the Aeneid, who was conceived during the affair with *Anchises.* Aeneas was the most illustrious son of Aphrodite by a human father and his story is worth recounting.

At times the powers of Aphrodite seemed to be quite limitless. It is recorded that even the mighty Zeus succumbed to her enchantments and fell in love with a Phrygian boy called Gannymedes, whom he had carried to Olympus by an eagle to satisfy his desire. Other gods were similarly affected at various times and formed sexual associations with men and women. In consequence Aphrodite became incautious and boasted openly before them of her power. Only the three virgin goddesses were safe from her! Zeus was finally forced to act in order to maintain his authority and turning the tables on her caused her to fall in love with the Trojan prince Anchises.

The love-struck goddess set off for Troy through the clouds, her colourful dress like a haze of fire, shimmering in the air. Arriving at Mount Ida where Anchises was tending his sheep, she was immediately surrounded by wolves, lions, leopards and bears who gazed on her in wonder. She in turn rejoiced in their ferocity and cast desire into their hearts whereupon the creatures withdrew into the shadowed valley and mated with their partners. Anchises was spellbound, and immediately felt the spreading of desire through his body. The involuntary nature of his desire was disturbing but it quickly passed and he saw only the burning beauty of Aphrodite who was herself under a similar spell. It was out of this whirlwind affair that Aeneas, one of the heroes of Troy was born. Poor Anchises however forgot Aphrodite's warning that he should keep their love secret and boasted of it to others, for which sin he was blinded by a thunderbolt from Zeus.

Priapus, sone of Aphrodite, attempted to offer violence to the nymph Lotis. To save her from dishonour the gods changed her into the plant lotus.

THE FOLLOWERS AND ATTENDANTS
OF APHRODITE

Aphrodite was attended by several divinities of varying importance among whom were **Desire, Persuasion** and **Fulfilment,** who represented the qualities signified by their names but had no distinct personalities. Quite different were the three **Graces,** *Euphrosyne, Aglaia* and *Thalia,* who acted as handmaids of the goddess, dressing and anointing her with perfume. These were minor deities in their own right, and most Greeks believed them to be perpetual virgins, though in some parts of Greece Aglaia was romantically associated with Aphrodite's husband Hephaistus. Some Greek writers represented them as daughters of Zeus and the nymph Thetis and others as the daughters of the sun and the dawn.

Their domain was over gentleness and refinement being particularly concerned with the fine arts, especially poetry, and sharing many temples with the nine **Muses,** for while the Muses could give inspiration to artists it required the Graces to give aesthetic form to their work. Nothing could possess charm and taste without their presence. They made women beautiful and desirable and made men handsome and wise. Through their benevolent influence the trees of the earth blossomed and when the right time came their fruit ripened and filled with delicious juices. On Olympus when **Apollo** played his harp, the Graces danced with Aphrodite and the Muses sang. All three Graces were extremely popular both among mortals and immortals because they spread joy and happiness. In Homer's Illiad they are represented as the keepers of the gates of heaven, which they open and close to create day and night and all the wonderful phenomena we see in the sky.

The deities around Aphrodite, were divided into complementary pairs; Desire would create the sexual appetites that Fulfilment satisfied, and **Eros** and his brother **Anteros** formed a partnership whereby the former initiated feelings of love while the latter punished those who were not responsive to such. At times Anteros might even separate mismatched couples. This interaction of positive and negative forces is representative of the belief of ancient Cypriots that creation begins at the point where opposing elements meet, and that explains why the goddess of love married the ugly Hephaistus and became the mistress of violent Ares.

Eros the winged assistant of the goddess has been represented in art and literature as a young man, as a child or even as a baby. The goat, the

Above: The Three Graces who dressed and annointed Aphrodite, by Regnault.
Below: Cupid and Psyche, sculpture by Canova.

Psyche and the west Wing Zephyrus, clay relief by Hary Bates.

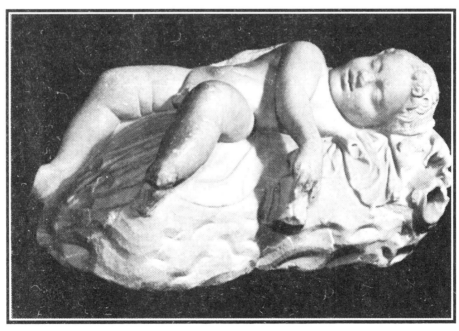

Sleeping Eros from Paphos 2nd Cent. AD (Cyprus Museum).

hare, the rose and the cockeral were sacred to him. According to Hesiod, he was the son of *Chaos* and accompanied Aphrodite on her journeys abroad. Other writers believed that he was the son of *Zephyrus*, (the west wind) and *Iris* (rainbow), a cruel child who caused disastrous relationships between gods, men and animals and enjoyed watching his victims suffer. In some places he was believed to be the son of Aphrodite herself; others still cast him as her lover. Whichever version is adopted the fact remains that he was the goddess's chief minister. He carried a quiver of golden arrows round his shoulders. When either a god or a man was wounded by one it had the effect of making him fall in love with the first living thing that he set his eye on. Aphrodite made frequent use of his power.

Eros was married to **Psyche** who only joined Aphrodite's entourage after the initial difficulties which we relate below. The story of Eros and Psyche shows the goddess in a malevolent mood.

Although Aphrodite was known and acknowledged by all, to be the fairest of all beings, human or divine, she herself was capable of experiencing jealousy on account of other women's beauty. The princess Psyche was an extraordinarily beautiful child, and as she grew and developed people began to say that no mere mortal could be as lovely as she, some went so far as to raise her temples, worshipping her as an incarnation of Aphrodite. Psyche herself was perfectly innocent and not at all vain nevertheless her fame spread and aroused the envy of the goddess who sent Eros down with instructions to wound her so that she should fall in love with the oldest and ugliest man that could be found. But when Eros arrived that night by the sleeping girl's bedside he was so taken with her beauty, that he leaned over to examine her more closely and, as he gazed at her, the princess, sensing a strange presence in the room, suddenly opened her eyes. The darkness prevented her from seeing Eros, but he was so lost in admiration that when she awoke he panicked and accidently pricked himself with one of his own arrows and so fell in love with her. Eros panicked for he realised that this new turn of affairs would certainly infuriate his mistress and that her fury would be accompanied by some punishment. The only solution he could think of was to abduct the girl secretly in the hope that the goddess would not find out so he carried her far off, winding his way through the night air to a secret palace whose existence was unknown. As an additional precaution he did not disclose his identity to the princess and warned her to make no attempt to find out. From then on he visited her every night in the palace, but left before dawn each time so that she was never able to see his face. Psyche was terribly happy and would have remained so, had not her two jealous sisters sought out the palace and confronted her. The stories she told them of her great joy only increased their envy and they contemplated how they might bring it to an end. They were fascinated by the thought of an anonymous lover, and decided eventually that this in fact was the very point at which they could cause the greatest mischief. They suggested to her that he might be some dreadful monster, simply biding his time before he murdered her. They had heard of a great serpent, they said, that had wrought much carnage in the local villages, and they advised her to find out as quickly as possible whether this was he. When they left, poor gullible Psyche trembled for her life and forgot the happiness she had enjoyed. That night, when Eros was asleep she got out of bed and shone an oil lamp on his face. Expecting the worse she was completely overcome with relief and adoration, but in her excitement her hand began to shake and a drop of hot oil fell onto the god's shoulders. Eros immediately woke, stung by his lover's lack of faith he disappeared, as did the room, the palace, and all its contents so that suddenly Psyche found herself alone and cold in a strange and desolate place.

Psyche was distraught and stumbled about in the darkness, running in this direction and that, until at last she came to a river where in desperation she attempted to end her life. But the god of the river was kind and would not close over her, but carried her instead quite gently to the opposite bank. It seemed to her, that perhaps all was not lost for if the gods were concerned enough to save her, they might yet restore her to her lover. Hopefully she began to search for a temple where she might hear some news of him. But she wandered from place to place in vain for no one had any clue to his identity. After many months she was on the point of losing hope again when she came across a temple dedicated to the goddess **Demeter** who advised her to seek out a particular shrine of Aphrodite's and there beg for mercy. This she did unaware that Aphrodite had already learnt of her affair with Eros and was bent on revenge. She treated Psyche with contempt and set her a number of impossible tasks to perform.

The first of these was to gather into separate heaps, the wheat, the barley and the millet that had been mixed together in enormous quantities in the temple stores. What was more she was given only a few hours in which to accomplish this, but as she was to give up in despair, an army of ants, sent by her beloved Eros, came to her assistance and completed the job on time.

Next she was ordered to collect the wool of a flock of *golden fleeced sheep*. This seemed much easier. She set about it with a light heart and skipped her way down into the valley where they grazed. But at the foot of the hill she came across a friendly god who warned her that all who tried to clip these wild sheep were killed by them and that rather than attempt to do this she should gather up the wool that the sheep had left on the thorny bushes near their pasture. Following his advice she succeeded in accomplishing this task too.

But now Aphrodite, thinking that Psyche must have had assistance set her something far more difficult. She pretended that she had been concerned for her beauty since the birth of her child and that the only way to recover it completely would be to use a magical ointment known only to **Persephone,** Queen of the underworld. Psyche must go and ask Persephone for some. Pool girl try hard as she might she could not think of a way to accomplish Aphrodite's orders, for it was well known that only the dead had access to the underworld. Once more at the very edge of despair, help was at hand. She heard the voice of Eros advising her how to gain entrance into the kingdom of the dead and what was more important, how to get out of it again. He warned her not to eat anything she was offered there, not to open the box that Persephone would give her.

So Psyche entered into the dark kingdom and though beset with terrors made her request known to its queen. Many times she was offered titbits to relieve her hunger and drinks to assuage her thirst, but faithfully she refused to touch any of them. Eventually Persephone placed into her hands a little casket containing the secret of beauty, and bade her to take it to Aphrodite. Psyche tightly clutching the precious object set off on the tortuous route that would lead her back to her own world but as she was proceeding on her way she began thinking about its contents and soon the idea crept to her that perhaps Eros would love her all the more if she were more beautiful. The desire to open it grew stronger by the minute until it completely overcame her. Finally she could not stop herself.

As soon as she raised the lid however, the spirit of sleep that Persephone had hidden in the box to guard her secret escaped and enveloped Psyche in a deep trance, so that she fell down and slept. This would have been the end of the affair, had not Eros out of his great love for her, pleaded with Zeus, that he should be allowed to marry his princess.

Zeus was moved by their cause and showed mercy, bestowing immortality on Psyche, making her like one of the gods. Furthermore using threats and promises he persuaded Aphrodite to change her mind and agree to the marriage. Later Eros and Psyche had a daughter whom they named *Delight*. Eventually Psyche was completely reconciled with Aphrodite and became one of her companions. Her story illustrates that the soul (Psyche), strengthened by love and purified by experience and suffering is capable of overcoming death.

Eros has been a popular subject with poets, painters and sculptors for many centuries. In contrast to Aphrodite's sensual images in art his are usually sexless and somewhat effeminate, not unlike representations of angels in Christian ikonography. A reason for that is that he was mostly thought of as an immature youth, not ready for a sexual life. Because he had special responsibility for homosexual love among men his statues were placed in the Gymnasia where young men took their exercises.

His most famous statue is the masterpiece created by Praxiteles for the town of Thespies where they celebrated a festival called *Erodidia* every four years. The festival included music and athletic competitions and became notorious for the nudity of the participants.

Eros and Psyche (Rome Capitoline Museum).

APHRODITE AND THE TROJAN WAR

The most famous of all Greek stories, and the central theme of the Greek imagination is the Fall of Troy. It is interesting that these events were precipitated by the decision of a man who did not give sufficient consideration to his judgement and by the vanity of the three goddesses, one of whom was Aphrodite.

And it is with Aphrodite that we begin, at the wedding feast of **Peleus,** King of Thessaly, and Thetis, a sea nymph. All the gods were invited, all that is except *Eris,* the goddess of strife, who was quarrelsome and destructive. She was furious at this plight and in order to spoil the feast for the others she threw down into their midst, a golden apple bearing the inscription *'to the fairest'.* This lovely apple of solid gold rolled along the floor until it came to rest before Hera, Athena and Aphrodite who happened to be standing together. It was immediately claimed by all three and a great quarrel arose between them. If Zeus had not intervened to part them there would have been a fight. Then they appealed for the decision of the other guests but they, being prudent, foresaw that any choice would leave the judge with two powerful and embittered enemies, so they politely excused themselves. The case was taken to Zeus himself who did not relish declaring on such a delicate matter, and ordered the goddesses to submit their dispute to the arbitration of the fairest mortal who at that time was prince **Paris,** the son of King Priam and Queen Hecuba of Troy.

"Go to Mount Ida", he said, *"to the son of Priam. He is a man of taste, well qualified to pick the winner".*

So the three contestants were escorted by Hermes to Mount Ida where Paris was tending his sheep. Now, although Paris had a reputation for being a fair and wise man, all three goddesses attempted to sway his favour by glowing promises of suitable rewards. In short, by bribery. Hera offered wealth and power, Athena wisdom and skill in war, but Aphrodite guessing intuitively at the man's special weakness, unbuckled her magic girdle by whose means she had poured desire into innumerable hearts, and promised him the fairest mortal in all the world for his wife. Paris hesitated between the three, but there was really little doubt in his mind as to the choice he would make, for while thought of fame, power and wisdom were attractive, beauty was immediate and, seductive. He awarded the prize to Aphrodite thereby gaining at one stroke a friend and two deadly enemies. Nor did he suspect that by doing so he was setting into motion a train of events that would lead to tragedy and disaster.

Paris was destined to destroy his family and his country. Before he was born a soothsayer prophesied that his imprudence would lead to the destruction of Troy. King Priam, to avoid this catastrophe, ordered a slave to kill the boy as soon as he was born but the slave felt sorry and abandoned him on Mount Ida where he was found and saved by local shepherds. As a young man he gained the respect of all shepherds on Mount Ida for his courage and skill with which he protected the flocks of sheep against wild beasts. He gained the affection of *Oenone,* a nymph on Mount Ida, whom he married and with whom he lived in perfect happiness. At the time of his famous judgement it seems that Paris had no idea that he was a prince of Troy, the son of king Priam and queen Hecuba.

Soon after Paris judged in favour of Aphrodite and gave her the golden apple king Priam proposed a contest and promised to reward the victor with the finest bull on Mount Ida, which was seized from the flocks of Paris. Paris was allowed to enter the contest and to compete against such famous Homeric heroes as *Nestor* son of Nereus, *Cycnus* son of Poseidon, *Polites, Helenus* and *Deiphobus* sons of Priam and the great *Hector.* He won the contest and his favourite animal, and his sister *Cassandra,* struck by the similarity of the features of Paris and those of her brothers, made inquiries and discovered that Paris was another of her brothers. King Priam acknowledged Paris as his son.

Time passed and the girl Aphrodite had promised Paris failed to appear, so growing impatient he equipped a fleet and set out to find her. He was accompanied on this journey by, amongst others, Aeneas the son of Aphrodite. The great winds bore them to the coast of Greece and up the river Eurotas, to the city of Sparta, where they were hospitably received by **King Menelaus** and his wife **Helen.**

Queen Helen, daughter of Zeus and Leda, was the most beautiful woman of her age. When little more than a child, she had been carried off by Theseus, king of Athens, from whom she was rescued by her brothers the demigods Caster and Pollux. She then married Menelaus, King of Sparta, whereupon her other suitors who were still deeply in love with her, vowed to guard her and her husband from any deeds of violence or injustice.

On the tenth day of the Trojans' stay in Sparta, Menelaus received an urgent message that his grandfather had died and that his presence was required at the funeral, so he sailed for Crete, leaving Helen to entertain the visitors.

The following day, the Trojans also decided to leave. Bidding farewell to Helen they set off in the direction of Salamis, but having sailed only a little way dropped anchor and returned under cover of darkness. That night they abducted Helen together with her baby son and carried them off eventually to Troy. Aphrodite was instrumental in this, for she had cast a spell on Helen which caused her to believe that Paris was in fact her lately departed husband. Peitho, Goddess of Persuasion, and Eros, whose powers are known, were also implicated.

Having achieved this ambition, Paris sailed first to Cranae and spent the night with his newly captive wife. He was hardly able to tear himself away from his beautiful captive. On they sailed towards Troy but the following day a violent storm interrupted their voyage and they were pleased to find shelter in Cyprus, which was rather off their course. Because of this they made for Sidon next, where Paris, still intoxicated by his success, murdered the local king and plundered his treasury to provide presents for Helen. Then once more they set out for Troy and eventually reached home by way of Phoenicia. Priam, whose own sister had been carried off to Greece by Hercules and forced to marry Telamon, welcomed this opportunity to pay off old scores and gladly accepted Helen into his household.

In the meantime, Menelaus, having been informed of the recent outrage, made all speed for home, and began to make preparations for a retributive war. His cause was acknowledged to be just and all Greece took arms on his behalf, his own brother Agamemnon being chosen chief of staff of the combined forces. Agamemnon went round recruiting allies. He attempted to involve **Cinyras of Paphos** in the war by sending Talthybius, Odysseus and his own brother the aggrieved Menelaus, to Cyprus. Cinyras promised to help but when the Greeks left he sent only one ship as token assistance. To appease the anticipated wrath of the recipient, Cinyras also made a personal gift to Agamemnon, that of a magnificent breastplate, whose description may be found in the 'Iliad'. But the Greeks were too preoccupied with their own preparations to consider taking any penal action so Cyprus remained in peace and increased in prosperity.

As for the Greek allies, they gathered at *Aulis,* in north-eastern Greece where Agamemnon began his campaign by capturing Tenedos, a port guarding the approach to Troy. From here he progressed to Troy itself and sent an embassy, under the flag of truce, to demand the return of Helen. The demand was refused. The Greeks then attacked Troy.

So the war started and it soon became obvious that the two sides were equally matched; battle after battle, sortie after sortie proved inconclusive. Though losses were heavy and the armies found themselves drifting into the second, then the third, then the fourth year and all without any significant progress by either side. The gods were equally divided on the issue; Hera and Athena abetting the Greek cause while Aphrodite, her lover Ares, and Apollo supported Troy. Others involved were Poseidon, Hephaistus and Hermes on the Greek side and Artemis and Iris of the rainbow, together with Xanthus, the river god who was also called *Scamander,* on the Trojan. Zeus remained aloof most of the time but his sympathies lay with the Trojans rather than the Greeks. As for Thetis, though she remained on the fringes of the action, her son Achilles was fighting for Agamemnon so she naturally extended a protective hand to him now and then.

Unhappily, Aphrodite though not without courage was no match for others in warfare and was twice wounded. Once she was struck by a Greek arrow and had to resort to Olympus and the healing ointments of Dione when Zeus, concerned for her safety, advised her to stick to what she knew, namely the art of love, and leave the fighting to those who were more suited to it. But she had her commitments to Paris and Aeneas, so she ignored his warning and returned to the fray. Though she failed to influence the final outcome of the war she managed to give effective help to individual Trojans at times of mortal danger.

The following incident tells of one such occasion.

The war now being in its ninth year, Paris was persuaded by his brother Hector to end it by arranging an individual contest between himself and a volunteer from the other side. So Paris stepped forward and declared that he would meet any Greek in single combat so that the issue might be settled once and for all. Menelaus, glad of this opportunity to avenge his wrongs accepted the challenge at once, but when Paris saw who was to be his opponent, he was struck by fear and guilt and tried to slip back into the company, terrified. Then Hector, his brother, the greatest hero of the Trojan forces, heaped abuse on him and shamed him into reassuming his position on the field of combat. All the men cheered this as they were sick and tired of the continual slaughter and lack of results and the agreement was solemnised with oaths, wine and the blood of a lamb.

Helen herself joined the Trojan king on the city wall to witness the contest, her heart by now being fully on the side of her former husband. Indeed she had grown to despise Paris once the spell of Aphrodite had worn off.

The two rivals took up their positions in no-man's land and faced each other with sword and spear. Paris, having won this right by lot, threw his spear first and struck Menelaus' shield but failed to pierce it.

Menelaus after a short prayer to Zeus, cast his and broached his opponent's spear and breastplate. But Paris twisted and turned his body so that the point only grazed his side. Next, Menelaus drew his sword and struck his enemy powerfully on the helmet ridge, breaking his sword in the process, but knocked Paris over. This was enough to give the king a second's advantage and he leapt on Paris furiously, seized him by the crest of his helmet and began dragging him towards the Greek lines. That would have been the end of Paris had not Aphrodite chosen this time to intervene. Invisible, she stood next to Paris and wrapping him in a dense cloud removed him from view of the spectators and of Menelaus, dropping him some distance behind the Trojan line. The astonished armies concluded that Paris must somehow have fled and were disgusted by such cowardice.

Menelaus rightly claimed his victory and his wife and would certainly have been awarded both, but just before a final decision was reached the Trojan Pandarus, being misled by Athene who did not want Troy to escape the doom her vengeance demanded, fired an arrow at Menelaus and wounded him. This treachery infuriated the Greeks who spontaneously fell upon the Trojans in force, thus robbing Menelaus of his victory.

The day was not finished and urged on by Agamemnon, battalion after battalion of the Greek soldiery swept into battle, forcing Hector and his Trojans to retreat in disarray. Indeed the Trojans suffered the greater losses and the gods flocked from Olympus to add their weight to one side or the other in the crisis. Athene was personally responsible for the death of many Trojans including her unwitting tool, Pandarus, and she also contrived to injure Aeneas who would have perished had not

Aphrodite protected him from further harm by rendering him invisible.

But the battle was dominated by one man, the *Greek Diomedes.* First he attacked Aphrodite and cut her hand at the base of the palm causing her great pain and forcing her to flee the field to the peace of Olympus, leaving Apollo in charge of her son. Next, when Ares burst vengefully on the scene and wreaked havoc among the Greeks, Diomedes confronted him, chariot to chariot and wounded the god of war severely in the belly, whereupon Ares let out a yell so loud that the mountains trembled. So Ares too was forced to retire from the scene. Of course Diomedes had not achieved this without divine assistance, for it was Athene that had manoeuvred their meeting in the first place, and had diverted Ares' spear from its course so that it landed harmlessly in the dust. Nevertheless Diomedes had already been wounded twice so his actions showed great courage. He was to be a scourge to the Trojans throughout the war and returned safely to Argos, his kingdom. But Aphrodite would not let him off so lightly and in revenge for her injury, stirred up trouble in the land and made his wife unfaithful to him so that at last Diomedes left his home in despair and died in weary exile.

Other men notable on the Greek side were *Teucer, Nestor, Odysseus, Aias* and of course *Achilles,* who in fact had quarreled with Agamemnon at an early stage of the war over the possession of a captive girl named Briseis; so his decisive contribution was not felt until the last stages of the war. It was at this time that Paris was wounded and retuned to his first wife *Oenone,* whom he had abandoned for Helen. She possessed healing powers but having been deeply hurt by his rejection of her, found it impossible to forgive him and withheld her aid so that Paris grew weak and finally died. But Oenone was unable to live on after his death for she had loved him very deeply, and shortly afterwards she hanged herself in a fit of remorse.

On Paris' death his brother Deiphobus claimed Helen's hand as of right and forced her to marry him, but this was not to be a lasting state of affairs, for that cunning artifice, the **wooden horse** was already in construction behind the Greek lines.

This had been the idea of one *Calchas* who was an inspired prophet. His plan was to build a gigantic wooden horse whose middle would be hollowed out so as to accommodate a large number of fighting men. The horse itself was to be constructed by Epeius with the help of Athene.

When the horse was completed the Greeks chose their finest warriors to man it, they burned their wooden huts and sailed for Tenedos. The battle ground was left deserted save for the horse. The Trojans were suspicious at first and standing around it debated what to do. Some said they should burn it, others wanted to hurl it from the rocks, but in the end they agreed to dedicate it to Athene. Then they turned to mirth and feasting believing the war to be over. Apollo's priest Laocoon, warned his Trojan countrymen not to trust the Greeks, and struck his spear into the side of the horse but before he could convince them, two enormous serpents rose from the sea advancing at great speed, and killed Laocoon together with his two sons. The Trojans were convinced that the serpents had been sent by Athene to punish the priest and tried to make amends by dragging the ill-omened horse into their city demolishing part of the city walls in the process. Aphrodite, aware of the danger made one last attempt to save Troy. She cast another spell on Helen, who had been informed of the Greek plot, and made her betray the secret to Deiphobus. But he did not believe her and that very night the Greeks emerged from their horse and opened the city gates.

Aphrodite's spell this time lasted only an hour and when it wore off, Helen sat at the window of her bedroom and gave the signal for the newly returned Greeks to attack, whereupon Troy was inundated by hostile troops, and its people including Deiphobus and Priam, massacred. Very few Trojans survived the ensuing bloodbath. *Cassandra,* who had been prophesing the destruction of Troy ever since Paris had returned from Greece, was taken prisoner and was to be murdered in Sparta. Queen Hercuba all of whose children had perished was soon to meet a tragic end, being changed into a wolf. Andromache, Hector's faithful wife was sold into slavery and her children slain. Aeneas managed to escape after valiant resistance. Before he left the burning city he spotted Helen, alone, in the porch of Hestia's temple. Enraged that the cause of so much suffering should still be alive among the general slaughter he was determined to kill her, but his mother Aphrodite suddenly appeared and bade him to look after his own family who were in mortal danger. *"The destruction of Troy was not caused by Helen"*, she said to him. *"But by the avenging gods"*. Aeneas managed to save his son Asconius and his blind father Anchises whom he carried on his shoulders, but his wife Creusa was lost in the darkness and he could not find her. The family sheltered for a while on Mount Ida and young Ascanius returned to Troy to help a band of refugees. As for Aeneas after many adventures which took him to Delos, Crete, Carthage and Epirus he arrived in Italy where he married Lavinis, daughter of king Latinus, and settled in Lavinium, Rome's forerunner.

The Trojans and Latins adopted each others customs, laws and religion and were united under the single name of the Latins. But Aeneas did not live long enough to enjoy his new realm. He died in battle and Aphrodite persuaded Zeus to admit him to the ranks of the gods. Aeneas's father Anchises had died soon after their arrival in Italy and lay buried in Aphrodite's temple on Mount Eryx in Sicily. The exaltation of Aeneas set the pattern for the deification of Roman emperors, who claimed to be his successors.

Helen was discovered by Menelaus in her chamber. At first he intended killing her, but catching sight of her breast unveiled, he cast his sword away. So he took her home, though that journey too was not without incident for she was again abducted on the way, her beauty being still a strong temptation to others, and Menelaus had to seek her in Cyprus and Egypt. His arrival in Cyprus coincided with the death of his old friend and comrade in the wars, Demophon. When Menelaus himself died Helen was driven from Sparta and took refuge in Rhodes with its queen, Polyxo, whom she believed to be her friend. But Polyxo's husband had been killed in Troy and she held Helen responsible so, one day when Helen was bathing, the queen sent two of her servants, dressed as Furies, who seized her and hanged her on a tree.

Agamemnon on his return home was murdered by his treacherous wife *Clytemnestra* and a tragic blood feud ensued among the members of his family. Troy after its destruction, remained in ruins for a long time. Eventually a new town was founded but it remained a modest place until Roman times. The Romans felt a special responsibility towards Troy because they considered themselves as descendants of Aeneas. The leading Roman families claimed direct decent from Aphrodite herself, and for this reason, when Troy became part of the Roman Empire it was accorded special privileges and was treated as an independent state. The new Trojans were granted territories and exception from paying taxes, as a consequence of which their town grew and prospered; at the same time their old enemies, the Greeks, were occupied by the Romans and most of the cities that joined Agamemnon in his expedition against them lay in ruins or were reduced to insignificant villages.

Chapter Two

THE CINYRAID CYCLE

PYGMALION AND GALATEA

When **Pygmalion** was still a young man an incident occurred that was to embitter his consequent outlook and turn him into a hater of women.

At that time the law of his native city Amathus, dictated that all women should sleep with a stranger before their marriage because it was believed that if a husband happened to be the wife's first lover he would rival the gods in her affections. However the daughters of Amathus saw fit to defy the law, wishing to remain virgins right up to their wedding so in order to punish them, the goddess Aphrodite planted in them an insatiable appetite which caused them to lose all shame and offer themselves to all men indiscriminately. The citizens were bewildered and the women themselves suffered a variety of pains and discomforts as a result: they sweated, they itched, and were unable to sleep, they became irritable and scolded their husbands and children on any petty excuse. In fact they became downright unbearable both to others and to themselves, so that in the end some of them began to long for death as a relief. Some took to wandering in the streets at night half naked in the hope of attracting lovers, others roamed the woods and fields and resorted to venting their lust on harmless animals; it was very degrading. But their punishment was not yet complete, for Aphrodite, some say from motives of vengeance, some say from pity, finally turned them into rocks and piled them high at the foot of a hill near Limassol where they may still be seen. They go under the name of The *Propodites*.

Pygmalion was so disgusted with the women's behaviour that he decided to shun all female company and dedicated himself entirely to his work. He spent the days and nights in the silence of his studio, carving figures out of wood and marble, gradually improving his technique until his creations became so lifelike that they might have been mistaken for living men and women. But satisfaction eluded him for he was intent on producing a statue so perfect that it would eclipse even his most remarkable works. This intense ambition dominated all his thoughts to the total exclusion of any earthly friendship and brought him by degrees to the verge of insanity.

But Aphrodite, took pity on him and taking the form of a most beautiful girl, she appeared to him in a dream and inspired him with the vision he had longed for. When Pygmalion awoke he recalled his dream and relentlessly he set about his work in the hope of capturing her likeness, taking for his materials the finest white ivory, so smooth and white, that it might well have been taken for flesh, though of an unearthly kind. The statue that he carved far outshone anything he had made before; so flawless, so serene was this image, that for hours on end he sat watching it, willing it to move or speak. Thenceforth each day he would do this, and indeed at times he came to imagine that now her lips parted, now a hair trembled in the draught; sometimes life itself would seem to suffice her face and then he would stretch out his arms to touch her, but finding her cold he would relapse into listless admiration. Sometimes he kissed the statue and spoke to it tenderly. He rarely left her side, and when he did it was only to wander alone by the sea or in some distant valley where he would gather flowers, or amber or bright pebbles for her. He dressed her with expensive silks, put rings on her fingers and long necklaces round her neck. Pygmalion then placed the statue on a couch that was covered with cloths of Tyrian purple and called it his bedfellow. As time went on his passion for her grew and so did his melancholy.

Aphrodite was the guardian goddess of Amathus and her festival was celebrated with great pomp. Heifers with gilded horns were prepared for sacrifice, a dozen at a time, and the temples were filled with incense; priests wore their finest ceremonial garments and the laity milled around in the gardens and colonnades. On the day of the festival Pygmalion took with him an offering of great value, stood by the altar and prayed fervently that his statue be given life. Aphrodite, seeing his sorrow, was moved to help him. As a sign of her favour, the sacred fire burnt brightly and three times in quick succession a flame leapt into the air.

Gathering flowers from a nearby field he returned home to find a maiden standing where his statue had been. It was most certainly her, his ivory statue come to life. He was quite entranced by her beauty and stood, speechless, not knowing what to do or say; almost automatically he offered her the flowers. For a moment she was still, but then she stretched out her arms to accept the bouquet and he touched her skin and found it soft and warm. He wanted to touch her everywhere but she averted her eyes and would not look up at him, neither would she speak. Pygmalion, overcome, muttered a brief prayer of thanks, and taking his courage in both hands confessed his love for her and asked for her hand in marriage. The statue's face blushed as she turned again to face him and replied,

'Pygmalion, I know of your love and will indeed be your bride'.

Because of her fair colouring, Pygmalion named her **Gatatea,** which means *'the milky one'* and soon afterwards he married her. The goddess Aphrodite was present at the marriage. Nine months later Pygmalion's bride gave birth to a daughter, **Paphos.**

For centuries afterwards the day of Pygmalion's miracle was commemorated by the Amathusians with an annual festival at which the king of the city wedded an image of Aphrodite. Pygmalion was honoured as a patron god of the city and in later years people believed that he founded their city. The royal family of Amathus claimed to be his descendants and many amathusian kings were named after him, but it is not clear whether *"Pygmalion"* was a royal title or a proper name.

The kings of Amathus, like the kings of Paphos, were also high priests of the city. In addition to the statue of Aphrodite they married a priestess and consummated the marriage in the temple. This marriage used to last for a calendar year during which the chosen priestess represented the goddess and was served by other priestesses like Aphrodite was by the Muses. Round her waist she carried the key of her office which showed her superior position as the Keeper of the Temple. Children born from these temporary marriages were considered divine and one of them would succeed to the throne when it became vacant, the rest with their families and the families of their in-laws, formed the aristocracy of the city.

CINYRAS AND MYRRHA

When **Paphos** the daughter of Pygmalion grew up she married a Syrian named *Sandocus* who was then living in Cyprus, but it was in the land of Cilicia that the young couple made their home, and it was there that Paphos conceived and bore a son whom they called **Cinyras.**

There were legends attached to the birth and early years of this boy:

> Owing to his great skill on the harp, it was believed that he was in fact an illigitimate son of Apollo, the god of poetry and music. Pindar on the other hand makes him the god's lover. Nevertheless all agree in praising his wisdom, his ingenuity, his athleticism and his comeliness that caused Aphrodite herself to fall in love with him. Many fine qualities and outstanding deeds were attributed to him. The invention of diverse mechanical appliances, the introduction into Cyprus of metals, of weaving, of the potter's craft; and besides all these many miracles and supernatural powers. But setting these aside, the most enduring monument to his memory is the city of Paphos which he himself founded and ruled, and this is how that came about.

Cilicia had been struck by famine: the aged, the infirm, the young and their nursing mothers, these were the first to succumb, but soon the others saw that something desperate needed to be done. Thus it was that Cinyras and a small band of followers set sail in the hope of discovering some more fertile land and stumbled on the island of Cyprus, on the very coast where Aphrodite herself had been washed ashore.

How pleasant it was here among the fruit and vines; they were well content to settle in this place. So they built themselves a town, and in the centre of it erected a temple to Aphrodite, who, they believed had guided them to her birthplace, and Cinyras became the first king and high-priest of the new city, which they named **Paphos** in honour of his mother, and administered civil and religious laws to his subjects.

Cinyras was neither a tyrant nor a weakling; he set up a Council of Nobles to provide stability and enjoyed a peaceful rule. The power vested in the council was considerable; it could, if it wished, veto the throne, appoint the successor, or even in extreme circumstances depose the incumbent. However the executive decisions were left to the king. Cinyras pronounced judgements, declared policies, led the army into war, and, as this was his due, claimed the largest share of the spoils. All land owned by the state was available for his use; he had the seat of honour at feasts.

Under his rule the temple grew prosperous and Aphrodite showered favours on the city, on the island and indeed on the king himself, making him wealthy and giving him a long reign. By escaping the impoverishing consequences of the Trojan war Paphos became for a while the most powerful city in Cyprus. If all this could constitute happiness, Cinyras would have been the happiest of men, but his personal life was marred by ill fortune.

His son **Amaracos** had discovered how to extract the scent of flowers and make the most delicious perfumes from them. But he hoarded the secret glorying in his ingenuity and before long several of the gods grew jealous of his skill and coveted his delightful store. There was one special amongst them whose envy became an obsession and he finally murdered the young man in a field on the outskirts of Paphos, whereupon his victim was transformed into a herb, that we now call *marjoram*.

Cinyras was much saddened by the loss of his son but did not allow his grief to interfere with the smooth running of the state. However worse was to come. We have mentioned his extraordinary beauty as a young man, but as he grew older he gained rather than lost in attractiveness, for his features matured with the added dignities of his office and he looked the very image of a god. Unfortunately this aggregation of qualities was not lost upon those nearest to him and in **Myrrha** his own daughter a dreadful passion arose, far outstripping the normal affection of a child to a parent. Eventually she found a way to fulfil her craving for him.

Myrrha was a beautiful girl and suitors had gathered from many countries to seek her hand; the princes of Cyprus had come to vie with one another for the privilege of marrying her. Cinyras, faced with such a throng of suitors, did not know what to do and asked Myrrha to make her own choice. She remained silent, gazing at her father though he put this down to girlish modesty. When he asked her what kind of husband she wanted, she replied *"One like you"*. The king was flattered by this and praised her for being so devoted but the fact was that the girl could not choose otherwise.

She prayed to the gods in heaven that they should banish her sinful thoughts and extinguish the horrible desire, but none of them responded, not even Eros who denied the accusations of the other gods that it was his bow which had wounded Myrrha. At midnight, when everyone was asleep, Myrrha remained awake consumed by a fire she could not quench. She renewed her prayers and when she saw that there was no response and no end to her despair she decided to kill herself. She tied her girdle to the top of the door-post and fastened the cord around her neck. She was about to jump to her death from a high stool when the nurse woke up and saved her.

Some time later all the married women of Paphos went out into the fields to celebrate the feast of *Demeter*, the corn goddess, at which they all dressed in snow white garments and offered the goddess garlands made of corn ears, the first of the crops. The king's wife *Metharme*, was taking part in the rites which lasted for nine days and during which love-making was forbidden. So while the king's bed was empty of its lawful occupant Myrrha determined on her awful course. It was a particularly dark night, windless and starless. Had Myrrha been more careful of her passion she might have taken these and other things as omens, instead she stole from her room and padded her way across the courtyard.

The king lay asleep in his bed and so she came and sat down next to him and caressed his brow gently until he stirred, then like a succubus she seduced him. In the darkness he did not recognise her. Furthermore she said nothing so that her voice would not give her away. However she had been clever enough to anoint herself with some stolen perfume, such as the priestesses normally wore, and this was enough to reassure him. She meant to leave him then and to wash away the scent, so that she would be unsuspected when the king awoke. But in the heat of the moment she forgot her plans and clung tightly to her father and they fell asleep together. He woke first, recognised his daughter and in his horror and fury drew his sword to kill her. Having awakened to the noise of his rising, she cried out and fled into the palace garden, but being faster he soon caught up with her and was on the point of lifting his sword for the fatal blow, when Myrrha, who had fallen to her knees in a desperate prayer, began to change shape. The poet Dryden describes the event like this.

> *"The prayers of penitents are never vain;*
> *At least she did her last request obtain.*
> *For while she spake the ground began to rise*
> *And gathered round her feet her legs and thighs;*
> *Her toes in roots descent, and spreading wide,*
> *A firm foundation for the trunk provide:*
> *Her solid bones convert to solid wood,*
> *To pith her marrow, and sap her blood:*
> *Her arms are boughs, her fingers change their kind,*
> *Her tender skin is hardened into rind.*

And now the rising tree her womb invests,
Now, shooting upwards still, invades her breasts
And shades her neck; when, weary with delay,
She sunk her head within, and met it half the way.
And though with outward shape she lost her sense,
With bitter tears she wept her last offence;
And still she weeps, nor sheds her tears in vain,
For still the precious drops her name retain."

The king stood transfixed, his upraised sword gleaming in the silver light. Slowly he drew back and as he did so he became aware of Aphrodite sitting amongst the tree's branches, her sparkling gown spread across the leaves and shoots, her face calm and silvery as the morning itself.

"You Cinyras", she addressed him, "stand still and do not harm your daughter. Certainly she has done you wrong but she has been punished. You for your part, for you are not entirely blameless in this, must never damage this tree which is all you have left of her. No instead you must build an altar at her feet, and you must worship her daily, for so I command it. And if you do as I say some good may yet come from this matter".

This said the goddess disappeared leaving the king and the tree together in the garden.

When Metharme returned there was much sorrow at the fate of Myrrha, and coming so soon after the last tragedy, the loss of Amaracus, it was almost enough to drive them to despair. But their family was large, and as it was, after a long period of mourning they accepted their fate and resigned themselves to the will of the gods.

The goddess's instructions were strictly carried out. Three seasons passed and berries hung in purple clusters from the tree. One day the king was about to burn incense on the altar when the leaves above him trembled and parted and a baby boy of remarkable beauty fell from the branches into the arms. The child grew to be so fair that the Paphians regarded him with religious awe, paying him all sorts of honours and calling him **Adonis,** which means Lord.

King Cinyras had three other sons, apart from Adonis: the tragic *Amaracus, Kypros* who gave his name to Cyprus and *Curius* who founded the city of Curium. He also had five daughters, *Myrrha, Oresideke, Laogora, Breisis, Enna* who married the Homeric hero Teucre and *Laodice* who married the king of Arcadia Elatus.

Myrrha felt an unnatural love for her father Cinyras and crept into his bed pretending to be a priestess. Aphrodite stepped in and changed her into a myrtle tree to save her from the wrath of her father. Adonis was born from the myrtle tree nine months later.

Adonis, Aphrodite and Persephone (by A. Charalambides).

ADONIS

Adonis seemed, even to his contemporaries, to have the nature and appearance of an immortal. His conception, which of course was incestuous, parallels the cross-fertilisation of plants, and his legend, symbolises the life cycle of plants that germinate in spring, grow throughout the summer, suffer a temporary death in winter and come to life again with the return of spring. In infancy he has been dedicated to Aphrodite and placed under the care of the priestesses in the temple, where the votaries of the goddess paid him honours similar to those they paid her. As soon as he was strong enough to carry a spear, he began to hunt the wild animals that roamed free in the forests of Paphos. Aphrodite used to amuse herself watching him stalking his prey and felt proud of his exceptional skill, but was at the same time concerned about his total absorption in this activity, so she resolved to teach the adventurous youth the art of love. Disguising herself as a forest nymph, she intercepted him while he was out hunting and by artful sighs and maidenly blushes drew him to her. The ground beneath was deep in moss and lichen and as they lay down upon it, it blossomed forth in a profusion of violets. When she had sufficiently instructed him she revealed her true identity and from that time on they were inseparable, to the extent that Aphrodite began to neglect her duties on Mount Olympus.

Together they would roam the woods and ridges, accompanied by their hunting dogs, in pursuit of game and when they had caught as many as they wanted they would lie down and make love. This scandalised the more austere deities, who considered her dalliance unbecoming and soon their malicious gossip was half way round the world and could not help but come to her attention. This angered her and when *Clio,* the muse of History, reapproached her in person, she lost patience and retaliated by firing in the muse a passion for King Pierus of Macedonia, a passion which resulted in Clio's pregnancy. The child conceived through this spite-induced affair, Hyacinthus, was fated to be killed quite unintentionally by his lover Apollo, who then turned him into a flower.

Aphrodite and Adonis kept up their liaison in the face of growing disapproval and the jealousy of her former lovers. Among these last, Ares, the God of War, was especially envious and he swore to take revenge on the young mortal. He began by assuming the shape of a wild boar and terrorising the district of Paphos, killing and maiming the inhabitants with such brutal savagery that news of his horrendous deeds soon penetrated every corner of the hitherto peaceful island. Adonis could hardly resist such a challenge: his hunting instincts fully aroused, and ignoring Aphrodite's forbiddings, he took up shield and spear and set out to conquer the scourge of his countrymen.

He made his way to the hillside where the boar was known to dwell and here he beheld a terrible sight; a field strewn with macabre remains of unfortunate people. He looked around to see if he could recognize anyone he knew, but all the bodies were so mutilated that it was impossible to tell one man from another. Perhaps for the first time in his life Adonis was frightened for he had never seen such destruction, but taking his courage in both hands he walked boldly towards the largest clear space he could find and there he roared out his challenge to the boar. As if the creature needed any warning; he had been observing the young hunter's movements for some time from the inconspicuous entrance of his lair. He calculated the distance between Adonis and himself and having formed his strategy, charged at the youth with great speed, raising a thick cloud of dust around him. Adonis whose eye was as keen as an eagle's was blinded and when he came to throw his spear it was as though he were aiming at a crowd of phantoms. The boar, intent upon his course had only to make the slightest movement, no more than a twitch, to avoid the hurtling weapon and within an instant Adonis lay trampled and gored among the decaying dead. Ares bowed over his wounded rival and for a while could not help but admire the young man's beauty, but a vengeful satisfaction soon overtook this feeling and he departed without making any effort to save him. An owl who had witnessed these events quickly carried the news to Aphrodite, who rushed griefstricken to the scene. From the distance she could hear the dying groans of Adonis, and she wheeled her chariot, drawn by giant swans, through the trees and mountains of Cyprus. By the time she arrived it was too late to stem the flow of blood. She laid him on a bed of lettuce and exerted all her divine strength and knowledge to revive him. it was in vain. As soon as his spirit fled from the body, the fields, in sympathy, died up and the grass turned pale and the trees shed their leaves and ripening fruits. The lettuce on which his body rested acquired aphrodisiac powers.

As a lasting memorial to her lover Aphrodite sprinkled Adonis' blood with nectar and at the touch of this liquid the blood gathered and contracted into the shape of the flower we now call *anemone*. The name comes from the Greek word for 'wind', for its life is short and its petals easily shaken off by the gentless breeze. A white rose bush stained by the same miraculous mixture produced the crimson variety of roses.

Aphrodite was overcome with grief. She wept for many days and nights without ceasing so that even the sternest of the gods were moved and tried to comfort her, but she was inconsolable. Eventually she decided to plead with Zeus for the return of her lover, and he, being acquainted with her sorrow promised to ask **Persephone,** the queen of the underworld, if she was willing to release the young Adonis. But Persephone had herself fallen in love with the beautiful youth and would not let him go. When Zeus saw how deeply they both loved this mortal, to the extent that neither could bear to be parted from him he wisely ruled that for four months of the year Adonis could live where he pleased provided he divided the rest of his time equally between the two goddesses, and so it was done:

Persephone had him for four months as was her due, and Aphrodite for eight because he preferred to spend his free time with the Goddess of Love.

A Greek myth says that it was Apollo who transformed himself into the boar that killed Adonis as revenge against Aphrodite who had blinded his son Erymanthus when she caught him spying on her and Adonis bathing together.

The votaries of Aphrodite staged the death and resurrection of Adonis at an annual festival held on 25 and 26 March in Paphos and most other Cypriot towns. It was mainly a festival for women who made wooden and wax images of Adonis and Aphrodite, adorned them with aromatic plants and surrounded them with figurines of Eros, birds and animals, and with cakes which ancient Cypriots used to make for the dead. These preparations for the festival are familiar to those who have witnessed preparations for Easter by the Greek Orthodox church because they are so similar.

On the first day of the festival effigies of Adonis, made to look like corpses prepared for burial, were carried in procession to the seashore by wailing women who threw them into the sea. Other items thrown into the sea at Aphrodite's birthplace included flowers, green branches of the Myrtle tree and pots of plants specially grown for the occasion. Some of these objects were placed on tombs of Adonis which existed in several Cypriot towns. By these demonstrations women showed that they shared the grief of their goddess who had lost her lover but at the same time they were taking part in an agricultural rite, the shedding of tears being necessary for the fertility of the earth. (Sowers used to simulate mourning Aphrodite as they cast seed in the ground to die so that it may grow again as corn). The items thrown into the sea were meant to act as charms to produce rain and ensure a good harvest.

Hymns and elegies chanted by women mourners of Paphos were numerous and long. Tradition has it that these were composed by king Cinyras himself who was a talented musician and song composer. No doubt some were brought to Cyprus by travellers and pilgrims from Babylonia and Phoenicia. It seems that the best singers received prizes for their performances; the daughter of *Argia* from Alexandria being one of the winners for her sweet voice according to *Theocritus*.

One of the hymns went as follows:

He has gone to the bosom of the earth,
And the dead are numerous in the land.
We are filled with sorrow, we stagger in gloom
In the month of your name.
You have abandoned your people.

Another hymn refers to the slaying of Adonis:

Beloved of Aphrodite, the temple is empty
Wise shepherd, why have they slain you?
The spirit of life is gone
We wail the wilderness without trees
We wail the corn without ears
We wail the river without willows
We wail the lake without fish.

By the afternoon of the first day of the Adonia the number of mourners increased with new arrivals from villages around Paphos and the ceremonies became increasingly rowdy and hysterical. The loud music of tympana (drums) and pipes, the singing and dancing stimulated the women into an ecstatic state which deadened feelings of pain and awareness of the physical world. They scratched their faces and inflicted wounds on their bodies. Once they reached this condition they believed that they had achieved divine inspiration, that their soul had established communion with the spirit of Adonis.

Women from the villages who liked to upset the town authorities marched through the streets with bare breasts and dishevelled hair, shouting obscenities and tearing their clothes to shreds. They must have been a frightening sight to innocent citizens who crossed their path! Many of them shaved their heads as a sign of mourning, those who could not bring themselves to make this sacrifice were forced by tradition to offer themselves as prostitutes for a day and dedicate their earnings to the temple.

The second day of the Adonia was happier. People celebrated the resurrection of Adonis with animal sacrifices, feasting and praying.

In the town of Marium, where Adonis shared a temple with Aphrodite they celebrated the Adonia in the Autumn. It seems that in this town Adonis was a corn spirit rather than a god of vegetation in general and his festival was probably timed to coincide with the planting of corn. Marium was a less significant centre of worship than Paphos and its festival was a minor event by comparison, but it had some interesting peculiarities.

As in Paphos, the first day was one of mourning for the death of Adonis, and people ate only green vegetables; the women chewed garlic in order to repel the men's advances for both wine and sexual intercourse were forbidden.

The purification of the temple began at dawn:

Prayers were chanted, the walls and doors of the temple smeared with myrtle resin, and a lamb was sacrificed. This last was an act of exorcism; the creature was slayed and its hide used to mop up the blood which spurted across the temple floor. People avoided touching its flesh for that is where the exorcised spirits were supposed to take refuge.

The women brought flowers and aromatic shrubs and placed them on a bier inside the temple; while this was going on others were casting live doves onto a pyre in a specially constructed oven made to contain two separate fires, so that as the doves flew out of one they blundered into the other and were thus consumed. At some stage in the distant past they probably put people in there too.

After this people returned to their houses and lodgings and prepared small shrines using stone images of Adonis. These were placed at the entrances and surrounded by fruit and vegetables and cakes baked into phallic shapes. Every house in the town sported such a display. Then in the evening came the central event, the Gardens of Adonis. The 'Gardens' themselves were no more than a miscellaneous collection of gold and silver containers which were filled with decorative plants.

The women carried these, along with the Adonis figures, in a dark parade through the streets, weeping and wailing for the dead hero. Their breasts were bared and those who were not actually carrying anything beat themselves there in time with the lamentations.

There have been times when the women have become quite frenzied, and the city authorities thought it necessary to lay down strict guidelines as to the conduct of this demonstration. But in later years the procession would wound its way down to the sea without any violent outbreaks, where the Gardens were cast, to the accompaniment of wild prayers and even wilder songs, far out into the waves.

Later the fast was broken with a meal of pork. In this detail too the Marians varied from the rest of Cyprus. Other Cypriots would never dream of touching pork during the Adonia for they associated it with the boar not with the victim, but in Marium it was the other way round and Adonis was assumed to be incarnate in the pig; hence the sacrifice and devouring of the beast seemed to them perfectly in order. Visitors had more qualms about this than almost any other divergence from normal custom, although many did eventually eat of it. When the meal was ended the fat and bones were burned as a sacrifice on the altar.

On the second day the mood was far more joyful. Flowers were cast into the sea and they celebrated the resurrection of Adonis. There were animal sacrifices, feasting and mating: Aphrodite was reunited with her lover. A marriage ceremony was enacted between the High Priest, representing Adonis, and a virgin priestess who had previously been chosen to take the part of the goddess. This was accompanied by music and praying, and the witnesses sprinkled corn, figs and dried nuts over the couple's head and round their feet. Meanwhile a room was prepared, strewn with flowers and decorated with all kinds of vegetation, where the pair immediately consummated their marriage. Of course no one was present and the area of the temple where the chamber was located was sealed off, but in due course blood stains from the womb of the virgin were exhibited on a white cloth, the union was proclaimed through the town and people rejoiced for they believed that fertility was bestowed upon their lands by this act.

Bad harvests were always blamed on the sexual performance of the High Priest at this ceremony and any High Priest of Marium who proved unable to consummate his marriage either though old age or through infirmity was immediately replaced by one of his sons. The selection was done either by popular acclamation or through a hasty meeting of the Council of Nobles.

Adonis was unknown in Greece in the time of Homer and no mention of him is made in the Illiad or in the Odyssey. In later years his cult spread throughout the Greek speaking world and his importance as a god equalled that of Eros with whom he shared many attributes and characteristics. In the 7th century B.C. he was known on the island of Lesbos as is shown by a *Sappho* poem. Hesiod also refers to him in his writings.

Aphrodite and Adonis – (A print by Raphael Sadler 1610).

END OF THE CINYRAID DYNASTY

According to *Anacreon,* the poet of Ionia, King Cinyras lived for one hundred and sixty years, dying in peace amidst great wealth. He was buried in the Temple of Aphrodite which he himself had helped to build and is now remembered as the goddess's favourite priest and the recipient of her generosity. His successors who carried the title Adonis, in memory of his brave son, were considered the official lovers of Aphrodite and were also to be buried in the Temple, the whole dynasty lasting over a thousand years.

The decline of the Cinyraid dynasty began at the time of Alexander the Great. When Alexander swept into Syria and Palestine he received military assistance from all the Cypriot kings except **Necocles of Paphos** who ruled over a theocracy and refused to help a man who seemed bent on destroying states similar to his own Paphos, in the name of Hellenism. Alexander never forgave Nicocles for this and soon after occupying the port of Tyre he accused him of corruption and had him replaced by a puppet ruler Alynomus, whose claims to the title were quite spurious, having been nothing but a gardener all his life. This episode illustrates the contempt in which Alexander held his enemies and provides also a measure of his power. But human life is short and Alexander's particularly so. As soon as he died (323 BC, 13 June) the old dynasty reasserted its precedence and *Timarchus Cinyras* took over the kingdom, to be succeeded two years later by his son **Nicocles II** who ruled for a further ten years before the city fell to the Ptolemies.

The capture of Paphos by the Ptolemies was a catastrophe that may well have been avoided. After the death of Alexander the Great two of his former generals, Antigonus, who ruled Syria, and Ptolemy the ruler of Egypt, laid claim to the island of Cyprus. Following a great deal of intrigue, Ptolemy landed on Cyprus with a large army and overran all the cities (313BC) except Paphos, which he decided to spare, for he was sensitive to the religious feelings of the populace. The state of precarious independence was not to last however, for it came to the conqueror's notice that Nicocles Cinyras, the Paphian King, was secretly dealing with Antigonus, his rival.

Ptolemy took grave offence at this breach of faith and in punishment sent two of his most capable commanders, *Argeos* and *Kallicrates,* to capture and execute the king. Their forces surrounded the city and Nicocles was ordered to commit suicide.

At first he tried to save his life by profuse apologies, promises of allegiance, tributes and so forth, but seeing that his case was hopeless, he gathered up the remains of his pride and withdrew into his chamber and there hung himself, the last of the Cinyraid Kings of Cyprus.

His brothers then locked the gates of the palace, set fire to it and slew themselves. Over the crackling of flames and the screaming of the frightened women, the Ptolemies shouted to those remaining alive that they were prepared to grant safe conduct to the Royal women and children. They might have taken up this offer had not queen **Axiothea,** maddened with grief and beyond reason, insisted that her relatives refuse outright; so all the women followed her onto the roof of the palace where, watched by a crowd of citizens from the square below, they stabbed first their children, then themselves to death until only the bereaved queen was left standing. She strode furiously about the little pile of corpses lamenting each one until, seizing on a large discarded sword she too drove the blade deep into her heart and fell into the flames that by now had engulfed all parts of the building.

The fire was eventually subdued but there were no bodies found and it was up to the scattered remnants of the royal family to form a council and choose, in the traditional way, the eldest among them to be the high priest of the goddess. But the power had gone, the only office that remained to this man consisted of purely religious duties for the Ptolemies abolished the city kingdoms and placed the whole island under the rule of a governor; and thus it continued for nearly three hundred years until the Roman conquest in 58 B.C., itself lasting to AD 330.

This last named Nicocles II had introduced a number of reforms in order to appease the aggressive Hellenism of Alexander's successors*. He had built a temple to Hera and cultivated the worship of Apollo, both deities more representative of the new rather than the traditional Cypriot ways. His coins represented Aphrodite on one side and Apollo on the other. He had combined the priesthood of Aphrodite with that of Hera in spite of the fact that the two goddesses were legendary rivals. In effect these two gods were usurping the goddess of the island and it was no surprise to many people when the king came to a bad end. But Nicocles is remembered even now, as a small village (**Nikoklia**) standing on the original site of Paphos bears his name.

* *The administration of the kingdom 7 miles to the west where Paphos harbour now is. The new town was called NEA PAPHOS and the old kingdom as PALEAPAPHOS.*

Eleven years after the conquest of Cyprus by the Romans, Mark Antony gave the island to Cleopatra as a gift. Cleopatra, like all the Ptolemaic queens of Egypt, considered herself to be the personification of Aphrodite so in this respect the gift was perfectly appropriate but the arrangement lasted only a few years. When Cleopatra and her lover committed suicide in 31 B.C. the Romans took control once more and gave the priesthood of Paphos to the local branch of the Ptolemaic family as compensation for the loss of their realm. The religious power of the new High Priest extended over the whole island but was centred in Paphos.

With the appointment of the first Ptolemaic high priest the association of the Cinyras family with the temple was terminated. The Ptolemies administered the temple until Christianity became the dominant religion in Cyprus.

During the Roman period the temple of Aphrodite was patronised and protected by the Roman Emperors but with the spread of Christianity in the 2nd century AD its importance began to decline. For a period Christianity and paganism co-existed amicably and influenced each others practices. The Christians injected a measure of dogmatism into the cult of the goddess of love and the pagans influenced Christianity through their myths and legends, and their magnificent ceremonies. Roman mosaics in Kato Paphos show Dionysos who had become a very important god in the pagan pantheon from the 2nd to the 4th century A.D., as a child sitting on the lap of Zeus with a shining halo over his head. This image was obviously borrowed from Christian ikonography and indicates that the new religion had an influence on the old, contrary to the view that only the old religion influenced the new.

In the 4th century A.D. paganism was proscribed throughout the Byzantine Empire. The great temple at Paphos was converted into a Christian church, only to be destroyed by an earthquake a little later. The curved stones of the temple were used to build a basilica and the Byzantine castle of Kato Paphos. In the 9th century A.D. a church was built on the site of the temple and the sacred Black Stone, the chair of Aphrodite, was cemented into the wall. It can now be seen in the Kouklia museum — next to the ruins of the temple, but before it was transferred there childless women used to visit the wall, to touch the divine seat believing that they would be cured of their sterility.

For around 1500 years, from the time of King Cinyras until the Christian era, the Temple has remained a centre of intellectual and spiritual life, a meeting place for people of all countries, its fame ensuring that Aphrodite would forever be associated with Cyprus and Paphos.

58

SACRED PROSTITUTION

Cinyras had introduced sacred prostitution as part of the cult of Aphrodite and the temple in Paphos was famous for the large number of its beautiful priestesses. It seems that the example of Paphos was followed by other Cypriot towns and a custom was established which obliged women to offer themselves to strangers before marriage. Similar customs prevailed in many other Middle Eastern countries where mother goddesses like Aphrodite were worshipped.

The length of time women served in this capacity varied from place to place. In Paphos at first they only entered the temple when they had lost their virginity but it seems that at a later stage, probably after their marriage, they served the goddess as sacred prostitutes for one day per year. The same custom forced the women of Phoenicia to make themselves available in the temple on a regular basis. Amorite women, as we are informed by the Bible, sat in fornication by the gates of the city for seven days and in Armenia women served the goddess *Aniatis* for a long time before they were allowed to marry.

It must be emphasised that the practice was a solemn religious duty the purpose of which was to communicate with the supernatural through the sexual act in order to re-activate the reproductive forces of nature.

The Middle East is susceptible to drought and famine, and in ancient times people faced the curse of child mortality as well as crop failures and animal diseases. They tried to deal with these disasters by evoking the life giving forces of nature through acts which related directly to procreation. It was believed that anyone having intercourse with a priestess of the goddess in charge of procreation would be rewarded. In discussing these matters we must also remember that prostitution was a profession free of moral stigma. Brothels existed throughout the world, some of which were run by the city authorities in the belief that they fulfilled educational and social needs.

In classical Greece it was fashionable for public figures to visit prostitutes and many statesmen, philosophers and artists associated with them freely and publicly. *Pericles* married the hetaera *Aspasia* and the famous courtesan Phryne had her statue at Delphi, the most sacred place in Greece. Athenian courtesans of the classical period were renowed for their beauty and their wit; they could play music and hold discussions with great philosophers like Socrates. *Phryne* posed for her lover Praxiteles and helped him create his most famous statue, **Aphrodite of Cnidus.**

She also posed for the painter Apelles for his best known painting, Aphrodite Drying her Hair. Many professional prostitutes used to contribute part of their earnings to the temple of their guardian goddess. In a poem by Nearchos a young prostitute who had just entered the profession promised Aphrodite ten per cent of her earnings if the goddess helped her attract customers.

The priestesses of Aphrodite in Paphos, whose function was not entirely sexual, were trained in the rules of sacrifice, prayer and purification. They played prominent parts during the **Aphrodisia festival** *(see pages 101-106)* and took part in sacrificial feasts. When public prayers were offered to the goddess their participation in large numbers was considered essential. Priestesses were not required to possess any special qualities other than a willingness to carry out their duties conscientiously.

The usual source of prospective priestesses was the lowest class of temple ministrants, called sacred servants. Some of these servants were bought by the temple, others were dedicated to it by their parents when they were children. Their numbers ran into hundreds of both sexes and all were at the High Priest's beck and call. Normally they would be put to domestic or agricultural work, but some of the women were creamed off and trained as priestesses.

Another source of priestesses were the wealthy pilgrims with their slave girls. In ancient times men sought to gain the affection of their gods through bribery and to this effect the rich liked to buy beautiful girls on the slave market and dedicate them to Aphrodite. One example of this practice was the case of the Olympic champion Xenophon who had dedicated one hundred girls to the temple of Aphrodite at Corinth when he won his crown. At the end of the dedication ceremony, the donors stood up with arms out-stretched and palms turned expectantly as though in the act of receiving a present.

The women of Paphos served in the Temple for a day during the festival celebrating the reunion of Aphrodite with her lover Adonis at the beginning of spring. The daughters of king Cinyras himself served the goddess in this way which indicates that the rule embraced all women of a certain age, irrespective of social class.

The girls wore special head scarves and sat in a line inside the temple waiting to be chosen by a man. Men paraded up and down inspecting the girls and when one of them took their fancy they threw a silver coin in her lap and claimed her in the name of the goddess. The girls had no right to refuse a man and the silver coin went to the temple. The idea behind the rite was to immitate the reunion of Aphrodite with Adonis. For the same reason a sacred marriage between the high priest and a priestess was performed in the temple and was consumated in a chamber decorated with greenery. Children born of this union were considered semi-divine. These rites pleased the goddess of fertility who responded by activating the creative forces in nature so that the crops grew and the animals were able to reproduce their kind.

Girls who entered the temple to sacrifice their maidenhood were probably sixteen years old. In those days Cypriot men considered the act of deflowering a virgin dangerous and the temples of Aphrodite became crowded with girls waiting for foreign pilgrims. Some women waited a long time before they attracted a lover.

It is wrong to assume that all the temples of Aphrodite were palaces of licence and debauchery and that all her priestesses were part-time prostitutes. There were temples dedicated to Aphrodite where the priestesses had to be virgins and if any of them broke her vows of chastity she was punished severly. On one occasion a priestess was buried alive. Men who accused a virgin priestess of Aphrodite without justification were charged before a priest-judge who could pass very severe sentences including the branding of foreheads.

The office of the high priest at Paphos was hereditary. The high priest administered the temple with the assistance of a number of priests who, if one is to judge from their appearance in sculpture, were terribly effeminate and wore highly decorative garments. Some of them were probably eunuchs like the priests of Attis who castrated themselves and exchanged their severed organs with pieces of female garments. The idea of eunuchs serving Aphrodite was based on the myth of Persephone, Queen of the Underworld, who fell in love with Adonis and wanted to keep him forever after his death. To prevent a rescue attempt she ordered that no male or female god, nor man or woman would enter her kingdom. However, a pious priest found a way round the order by agreeing to be dismembered and so place himself outside the two specified sex categories. Adonis was rescued and from then on eunuch priests were favoured by a grateful Aphrodite.

The high priest was also assisted in his duties by a leading priestess, shown on pottery bejewelled and luxuriously dressed, with a key hanging from her neck to show that she was the keeper of the temple treasures. She was probably appointed for a year during the Aphrodisia Festival and was served by other priestesses as if she were a goddess. We do not know the

"The hetaira" was dedicated to serve the Goddess. Here she is shown playing her flute to Aphrodite – c.460BC (National Museum of Rome).

official title of this lady but her office must have been the highest a priestess could aspire to.

Priestesses, with special talents, rose to become oracles of the temple. These girls, being the main channel through which the goddess spoke, were extremely influential and were consulted by government officials as well as by private citizens. They spoke in the name of Aphrodite after having been stimulated by some device into an ecstatic condition. The knowledge that matters of life and death depended on their advice ensured that oracles would take their duties seriously. The vagueness of some of their answers was not designed merely to cover themselves in case of failure but was due also to their reluctance to commit themselves lightly. If one is to judge from their popularity they seem to have exercised their duties well and to the benefit of those who sought their advice.

The temples of Aphrodite were usually on mountain tops to emphasise her connection with the skies or on high ground near coast lines to show her connection with the sea. One of her gifts to plant and animal life was the refreshing morning dew which came down to the hot valleys from her cloud hidden temples. Sailors believed that Aprodite had the power to calm the seas and prayed in her seaside temples for her protection. Long and dangerous sea journeys were usually undertaken in April, the month of Aphrodite.

The earliest sculptures found in the temples of Aphrodite were simple monoliths in the shape of cones or pyramids. Some ancient writers believed that these stones were images of the goddess and others that they were her thrones. Some of them were carved but others were found in that shape. People believed that they had magical powers to influence natural events like rainfall, crop production and the reproduction of animal and human life. The conical shape is an obvious phallic symbol but it also relates to the belief that conical hills and mountains were the first solid forms to come out of the sea when life began.

During the Greek Archaic period sculptors gave Aphrodite human form representing her much like other goddesses: as a sensuous but serious and dignified female figure. She was fully clothed with one hand resting on her chest. Some idols found at various temples of Aphrodite show parts of the female body exaggerated but this was mainly due to the wish of some donors seeking medical assistance who wish to indicate to the goddess the area of their problem. For example, a lady who could not produce enough milk for her baby would commission a statuette which emphasised breasts and if she wanted to become pregnant she would draw attention to the area of her stomach. In classical times the goddess was at first shown half-clothed but later on completely naked, a fashion of representation which persisted right through the Hellenistic and Roman periods.

In the decadent days of Ptolemaic Egypt (of which Cyprus was an important province) and in Roman times Aphrodite was represented in painting and sculpture as a sensual woman dedicated to the pleasures of the flesh. These images coupled with the scandalous behaviour in some of her temples probably influenced the early Christian fathers to overemphasise the virtues of their own mother goddess, Mary, who was completely pure and a virgin.

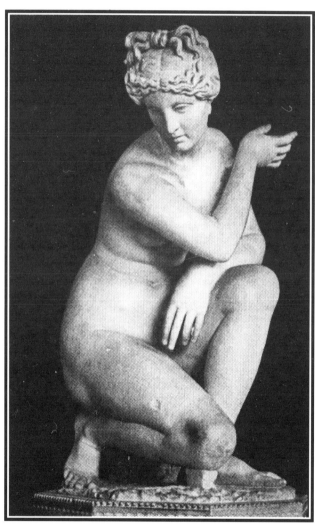

Aphrodite in her Bath (Vatican Museum).

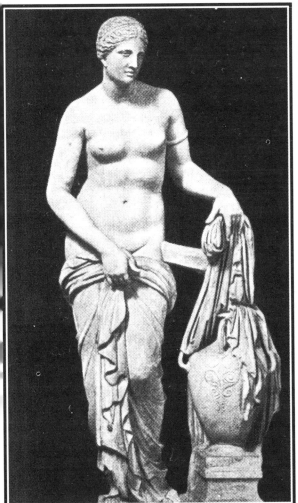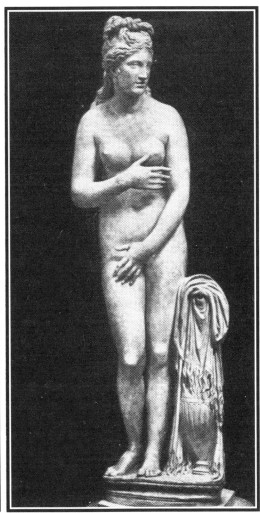

Left: Aphrodite of Cnidus – (Vatican Museum).
Right: Aphrodite of Praxiteles (Museo Capitolino).

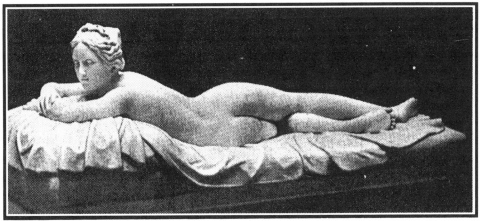

Aphrodite Resting by G. Schado – (Berlin National Gallery).

SACRIFICES

Ancient Cypriots were a deeply religious people. They accepted Zeus as "the father of gods and men" but their special affection was reserved for their native goddess Aphrodite whom they honoured with daily sacrifices and prayers. These honours, to varying degrees, were paid to all the gods including a group representing evil forces. To benevolent gods like the twelve Olympians they sacrificed in daytime, usually white animals, and when they prayed to them their faces and hands were turned expectantly towards the sky as if to receive a gift; a portion of the sacrificed animal was burnt on the sacred fire for the gods and the rest was eaten by themselves. In contrast, when people made offerings to evil spirits, it was to pacify them and to keep them away, the victim was black and its meat left to be consumed by the fire. When they prayed to these spirits their faces and hands were turned towards the ground as if they wanted to repulse an unwelcome presence.

Sacrifices were conducted daily at the temples of Aphrodite to provide food and drink for the goddess, who seemed to need it at least twice every day, and to establish contact with her in order to ask her for some favour. Offerings included bread, salt, cakes, vegetables, fruit and wine, as well as the meat of a goat, sheep, ox and other animals. The goddess was given only part of the offerings the rest going to the priests and temple staff.

At Paphos the main altar was reserved for *"pure"* offerings, that is to say those which did not involve slaughter but this was not so elsewhere in the building. The function of the sacrifice determined the nature of the thing offered; for instance at the beginning of each farming season the goddess's help was implored with bloodless oblations such as honey cakes, wine, fruit or vegetables. When crops had been gathered in, the same sacrifices were made as a token of gratitude. Normally they were placed on the altar or somewhere near it but other times they were thrown into the sea. Their contact either with the altar holding the sacred fire or with the sea in which Aphrodite was born, sanctified the offerings which were eaten afterwards. It was the belief that solid matter represented the body of the goddess while the liquids symbolised her blood.

Altars were of various sizes and materials and were positioned in a way that, when the door of the temple was open, the statue of the deity was looking towards it. The participants around the altar were dressed in their best clothes and had wreaths of myrtle on their heads. The victim, were it be a sheep, ox or swine, had to be in perfect health for abnormality displeased the goddess and there were severe penalties for those who offered faulty specimens.

Sacrifices were sponsored by the city authorities as well as by individuals who wanted some special favour or wished to consult the oracle of the temple. Public figures leaving office were obliged by tradition to sacrifice an animal to Aphrodite as a gesture of gratitude for blessings they had enjoyed during their term of office. Unmarried women who found husbands as a result of praying to Aphrodite also sacrificed to the goddess.

Sacrifices to Aphrodite were festive occasions with a diversity of entertainments financed by those who wished to carry favour with the goddess and as most sacrifices took place in the festive season there was a great appetite for feasting, singing and dancing. Some of the songs were commissioned for the occasion and their humourous content reflected the prevailing high spirits and the easy familiarity that existed between the goddess and her worshippers. Because the goddess was believed to participate in the feast in person an empty chair was kept for her next to the sponsor of the sacrifice.

As to the sacrifices themselves they were preceded by a purification ceremony: a jar of water was sanctified and placed by the altar, then the knife to be used was placed in a basket along with some corn and carried round the altar by the officiating priest to be similarly sanctified.

The priest then washed his hands in holy water and sprinkled some of it on the people. After this the victim was led to the altar and its behaviour observed; if it did not struggle back the omens were good and corn was scattered on its head and body. The priest then cut off some of the animal's hair, threw it into the sacred fire and dedicated the victim to Aphrodite.

In the event of a public sacrifice the priest would declaim aloud the reason for the sacrifice, but if the sacrifice was made by an individual, and was of a personal nature, the reason for it was whispered. At this point the priestess and women among the participants entreated Aphrodite's presence. The size of the flame produced by the burnt hair was an indication of the goddess's favour and indicated whether the petition would be granted or not. If it was of the correct size the head of the victim was drawn back so that its face turned to the sky and its throat was cut. The blood shot into the flames, and the worshippers cheered. Powerful animals were first stunned with skilful blows on the head from the blunt end of an axe. The animal was then skinned and carved, and the thigh bones wrapped in fat and burnt on the sacred fire while libations of wine were poured over them. The flavour of the burnt pieces and the wine were believed to reach the goddess wherever she was.

Sacrificed animals were supposed to be inhabited by good spirits and so their innards, the liver the lungs and the heart were first to be roasted. They were to be eaten while the spirit was still present in them. Then other parts of the carcass were cooked to provide a common feast for the goddess and her people. Normally male animals were offered to the gods and female ones to goddesses, but this rule was not followed at Paphos where Aphrodite would only accept males.

The priest who conducted the sacrifice was entitled to the hide and one of the legs of each animal but his assistant who struck the animal was not allowed to eat any of it and was paid a fee instead. Neither the priest nor his assistant had any spiritual standing, their only qualification was their ability to kill animals efficiently. If any meat was left over after the sacrifice people were allowed to take it home.

One did not have to be wealthy in order to find a suitable sacrifice. Inside the temple there was a table on which the votaries might place flowers, fruit, bread, cakes in the shape of animals, and other offerings of modest value. There was hardly anything which was unacceptable to Aphrodite from gold and silver to tools of artisans who were abandoning their trade. These were kept on stands, on shelves and on the floor around the shrine. Larger and heavier presents to the goddess were exhibited outside the temple.

Even human hair was acceptable as an offering to Aphrodite. The Queen of Egypt, Berenice, made such a sacrifice. She had vowed to give her hair to the goddess if her husband returned safely from a dangerous expedition. When he did, her locks were placed in the temple of Aphrodite but soon afterwards disappeared and the astronomer Conon reported that Zeus had carried them away and had formed a constellation of stars out of them.

When a town was threatened with catastrophe and in order to avert it people made unusual and painful sacrifices to Aphrodite. The people of Locri in Sicily promised to prostitute their daughters and wives in the temple of Aphrodite, every year, on the day of her festival, if they won the war against a neighbouring city. Unlike the votaries of Aphrodite in Paphos and other places the people of Locri considered prostitution as a great sacrifice. When they did win they tried to go back on their promise but their leader, as a kind of compromise, ordered that a selection of three hundred women perform the sacrifice on behalf of all the others.

It appears that human sacrifices were offered in certain places. At Salamis and Curium for example human victims were presented annually. Other towns resorted to it in extreme circumstances, and these were demanded by Aphrodite, as vengeance for some great sin committed by the inhabitants. Corpses have been found alongside certain kinds of altars with drains in them presumably to allow the blood to run off; these may have been sacrifices of this type — alternatively they may have been those of captured enemy soldiers used for that purpose. At Lapithos, in the Northern coast of Cyprus, skeletons of men bound hand and foot were discovered at the entrances of tombs, possibly slaves that had been sacrificed on the death of their masters, and who were intended to serve as door-keepers or scapegoats.

These practices were brought into Cyprus by Teucer at the end of the Trojan war. He founded the city of Salamis, where once a year a human victim, led by youths, was made to run three times round the altar of Aphrodite whereupon the priest thrust a spear through his throat. The corpse was then thrown onto a fire and burnt. Such victims were supposed to atone for the collective sins of the city populace and to deliver them from the perils of disease, famine or the wrath of the gods.

However, from an early age human conscience revolted against such cruelty and the rite was changed in various ways. In Curium they justified the act by selecting a criminal (that is, somebody no longer fit to live) as victim and he was thrown over a cliff into the sea. At Amathus they avoided the issue by sacrificing strangers only to Zeus Xenios but the custom offended Aphrodite and the offenders were changed into bulls. In other towns they simply simulated a human sacrifice or they replaced human victims with animals. The practice was abolished during the reign of the Roman Emperor Hadrian. King Deiphilus of Salamis was the first of the Greek leaders to substitute oxon. It is interesting that oxon should have been considered suitable, because to this day many of the older Cypriot peasants attribute human qualities to the creature and some of them refuse to eat beef.

A sacrificing Priest.

DIVINATION

Ancient Greek Cypriots believed that divination was one of the benefits given to mankind by the hero Prometheus and as a science it was considered of the same importance as metal-making, arithmetic and astronomy. In the course of time the temple of Aphrodite in Paphos accumulated a mass of information dealing with every augural phenomenon. This information was documented and classified and was passed on from one generation of priests to the next. Consultations with the oracle were held during festivals and every Friday which, being the day of Aphrodite, was deemed to be lucky.

One of the methods used was to pour oil, provided by the suppliants, onto cold water and then read the course of future events in the shapes made by the separated oil. There were other methods but the speciality of the oracles of Aphrodite at Paphos was hepatoscopy, which means the examination of the liver of a sacrificed animal. This art was introduced to Paphos by Tamiras who came from Cilicia and set up as a very successful fortune-teller in Paphos. After his death his practice was inherited by other members of his family who continued to perform his art until they came into conflict with the royal family of the Cinyraids who could not tolerate a second centre of influence in their city and a source of enormous wealth to be controlled by another family.

According to Tacitus the two families agreed to share the administration of the temple of Aphrodite and they did this for a while, but later the Cinyraids claimed that it was unfair to themselves and insulting to their royal dignity to share responsibilities with foreigners. They had the Tamirades banned from the city and retained the right to select the oracles of the goddess from among themselves and among the priestesses of the temple.

Omens in astrological phenomena, and those read in the liver of sacrificed animals, usually concerned the king, high officials and the state; omens in dreams, unusual observations etc. were of concern to private individuals. The direction, size and colour of the vains in a liver were crucial factors in hepatoscopy and were interpreted with reference to their resemblance to objects or events: Those on the right hand side were favourable, those on the left unfavourable. The Paphian oracles were very highly regarded which would seem to indicate that their forecasts were generally accurate, a reasonable supposition if we bear in mind that these

70

oracles were in uniquely advantageous position to gather information. After all temples were meeting places for all ranks of society. People explained their situation quite comprehensively before asking for advice, then again the psychological effect of a favourable forecast often ensured that it would come true.

It seems hepatoscopy at Paphos was practised by priests rather than priestesses. Tacitus in his history gives us the name of the priest Sostratus, who advised Titus during his expedition against the Jews. Titus sailed to Cyprus to visit the famous temple and to consult the oracle of the goddess. He was told that there were no obstacles in his way and that his journey will be happy. Then Titus sacrificed many animals and asked about his personal fate. The priest Sostratus, seeing that all the victims showed happy signs and that the goddess was favourable to his expeditions gave Titus an encouraging but short answer as was the custom, but later he talked privately to Titus and revealed the future. From Cyprus Titus sailed to Judaea, in 70 AD where his military superiority triumphed. The Jewish state was shattered, Jerusalem destroyed, the Temple fallen. Those that managed to escape did so. The others, mainly the able-bodied were sold as slaves. Some Jews from both categories found their way to Cyprus.

Priestesses selected to become oracles of Aphrodite in Paphos had to be highly imaginative and secretive because their prophesies depended on these qualities. Like the prophetesses of Apollo they stimulated themselves into an ecstatic state by chewing leaves of plants containing narcotic substances or by inhaling smoke produced by these leaves. When they reached a state of inspiration or divine madness their faces became wild and their bodies trembled; their hands moved as if out of control and made unnatural gestures. Sometimes the oracle fell to the ground and froth came out of her mouth. People explained the unnatural behaviour as the result of a divine and powerful spirit entering a frail human body. Sounds made by an inspired oracle were considered to be the voice of the goddess and although these could be poetic and rhythmical their meaning at times was so obscure and mysterious that they had to be interpreted by a specialist priest. A fair amount of time was needed for interpretation and this was used by those in charge to reflect and take advice on difficult questions.

Apart from the official oracles there were freelance magicians who claimed to know the secrets of *Orpheus* and *Musaius*, children of the moon and Muses, and to perform their magic art according to divine instructions. They attended the festivals and hawked their talents in the market place as seers, interpreters of dreams, or healers.

A great deal of other, semi-religious magic also took place whose purpose was to compel the goddess to respond to somebody's request. Often the motive that lay behind these efforts were malicious; revenge, spite, greed etc. Alternatively they were used to exorcise evil spirits or to insure someone against a spell.

The popularity of oracles was partly due to superstition. Greek Cypriots believed that unusual events in nature were omens, and when these occurred they asked an oracle to explain their meaning. Their attitude to natural phenomena is understandable considering that their gods represented the various forces in nature. Omens were read in cloud formations, in the behaviour of animals and in many other ways. Human, animal, plant and geological monstrosities, as well as freak weather conditions were signs that a god had been angered and had to be placated with a sacrifice.

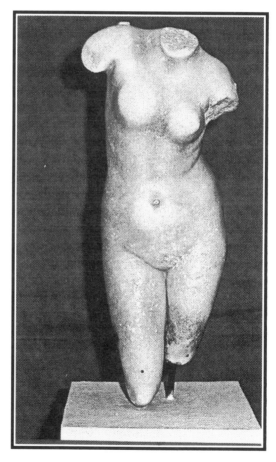

Aphrodite of Paphos/Greco Roman Period/(Paphos District Museum).

Chapter Three

THE TRAVELS OF BRONTEAS*

FESTIVALS

I am back at Aphrodisium again. I must admit I like the place more and more despite its filth. A disgusting smell of stale food and offal permeates my room. Nobody notices it here. If you mention it to them they look at you with startling eyes. But with all the festivities everyone is so cheerful it is hard to remain angry or even disgusted for long.

Their temple is dedicated to *Aphrodite Epipontid*, who calms the seas and looks after sailors. It is on top of a hill which is almost inaccessible. To reach it you have to follow a narrow footpath and negotiate your way through vicious thistles, loose stones that may throw you off your balance and drunken sailors singing their rawdy songs.

Yesterday I saw the pigs that are to be offered for sacrifice tomorrow. All twelve looked in excellent condition. (In a town like this it is scarcely surprising!) I hope it turns out well for them though. The last two years have produced rather poor harvests.

aving walked for a week in delightful weather I am as brown as an Egyptian, my skin hardened (especially the soles of my feet), my weight reduced and my strength doubled. One really should take more exercise.

* *BRONTEAS is a fictitious intellectual character but all events he describes in his travels are based on **documented** historical and mythological sources.*

I am a little surprised with **IDALIUM.** I had heard something about Idalian procedure but was not prepared for this. Let me start at the beginning. I arrived on Monday at about lunch time, so naturally the first place I inquired after was an inn. A slim and elegant young man offered to direct me to a suitable place and I walked along with him through some groves until we came to a large house set in a small but extremely ornate garden. *'This'*, he spoke in light melodious accents, *'is my house. You are welcome to share a meal with us'*. So I followed him inside. The house too was decorated, liberally strewn with flowers, pitchers of wine, small statuettes. It was all very delicious but somehow strange. Imagine my surprise when, as my host called out some names, there appeared at various doorways the strangest assortment of creatures:

A being whose limbs were covered in strips of light grey fur and from whose snouted head there protruded two enormous ears; another smeared in grease and paint, wearing pink garments, a piggish mask and from behind whom there peeped a curling little piggish tail. Was I dreaming? Then a third creature appeared. He was less startling than the others though in his own way just as strange. A man, sporting a full grown black beard and thunderous eyebrows, slunk into the room, attired in a filmy female dress and exuding a most heady perfume, he, seeing my confusion, hastened to reassure me. In a masculine voice (I believe he had a cold) he explained that all this masquerade was part of the Spring Festival. His two daughters, normally charming creatures he assured me, were assuming the identities of a rabbit and a pig respectively. He himself dressed as his wife and his wife (the elegant young man who had brought me here) was wearing the clothes of a man. Of course when he said this the whole thing fell into place.

The idea of changing sexes at festivals is not uncommon; it relates to the idea that man is engaged in an eternal struggle to purify himself from an inherited sin. According to this idea the Titans killed and ate Dionysus when he was a baby, except for his heart which was used by Zeus to recreate the young god. Zeus killed the evil Titans with a thunderbolt and out of their ashes sprang man with two sides to his nature, one good inherited from the consumed parts of Dionysus and one bad inherited from the matter of the Titans. Changing appearances at the festival shows that people are ready to abandon their sinful selves and the ecstasy induced by music, dance and intoxicating drinks is an effort to reunite their spirits with the gods. It is a neat theory but my own view is that negative and divine forces exist in all living things and one cannot purify the one without destroying the other.

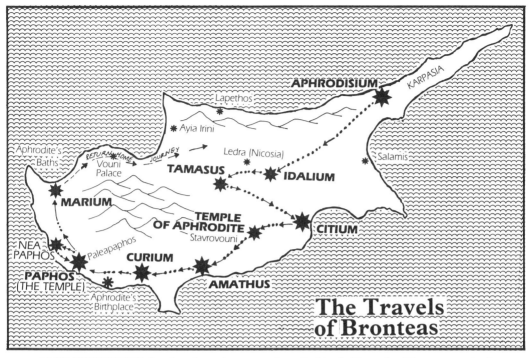

MAP OF CYPRUS *showing the main centres described in the Travels of Bronteas and other ancient places.*

Above: Votive sculpture in the form of a Human-Headed Bird.
Left: Votive sculpture of a woman.

But to cut matters short I enjoyed an excellent meal with good wine and found accommodation. Having expressed a desire to participate in the ceremony I was provided with an old costume of the mother's, anointed with perfumes, and was teased and petted by the daughters. My host then said the necessary prayers and the lot of us went back down to the town.

Here the festival was in full swing; people, creatures, running about doorway to doorway, laughing, singing, dancing. The family split up and I was quickly set upon by two locals who plied me with wine and scattered flower petals all over me. Don't ask me whether they were men or women! Thus the afternoon passed into a haze. I seem to remember the beautiful temple a little way out of town, some bright and glorious costumes, and indeed for a few minutes something very like a vision, a tall beautiful woman shimmering among the tree's impossible height.

After that it was bodies and limbs, beasts, birds and singing. Heaven knows where I rested. I woke in darkness in somebody's garden. There were people scattered about here and there. It must have been early in the morning for the sky was steadily growing lighter. I sat for a while with my head in my hands, then noticed smoke rising over the nearest houses, and heard music. I wandered across to find a great bonfire and a group of musicians warming themselves, idly plucking at strings and blowing down pipes, so I joined them. Eventually they produced some food which they were generous enough to share with me, and as the sun rose a crowd gathered in various states of undress, some clutching cloaks round themselves, in their hands they held remnants of the night's costumes. Then the priests arrived. They stoked up the fire and ordered the musicians to play. Now people began dancing, quite slowly and decorously round the flames, and as the music grew wilder they cast their costumes onto the fire. I soon got the hang of this and took off some of my own clothes (my hostess's I should say). They believe that mischievious and evil spirits inhabit people's clothes. All evil was to be burnt away. The naked body was to remain pure. The clothes were in effect atoning for last night's orgy! (Hence the disguise, it confuses the demons). I am sitting at my kind host's table now having drunk more wine than is absolutely good for me. Dare I suggest that the whole thing is only a pretence? An excuse if you like? Does the Goddess really approve? Still, the idea is rather clever.

Ceremonial Vase in the form of a hermaphrodite figure.

What can I say about **TAMASUS?** All our copper comes from here. Everything that can be is made of copper, from pans to plaques and jewellery. I have even seen copper facades and copper roofs —mostly green of course. But the chief attraction here is the Sacred Grove and the tree that produced the golden apples Aphrodite gave to Hippomanes to help him with his *"win or die"* race against Atalanta. Every time she was about to overtake him he threw one of these fascinating apples in her way to slow her down. In the end Hippomanes won the race and his bride Atalanta, but he was not to enjoy the fruits of his fraudulent victory, for soon afterwards they were both turned into lions by Demeter for daring to make love in her sacred cave.

I saw women queuing there for consecrated fruit. The priests administer these as a cure for childlessness. Apparently it is very successful. For me the place has great appeal. It is peaceful, well regulated and one does feel a kind of serenity radiating as it were from the groves.

I have been excluded from all the rites! Not for any transgression on my part, any ineligibility owing to poor preparation or lax morals, but because I am a man. The whole male population of Tamasus is excluded. So we sit here together in the market place pondering what could possibly be going on in the temple. Quite futile of course — nobody will ever know. Ah, but we may guess. There are all kinds of theories, most of them too disgusting to repeat, which show how little we men trust women. A part of me concurs with the general feeling. Women are less trustworthy and far more lascivious than we are.

However I am straying from the point which was one of masculine theories about female rites. Here is where the comic element comes in, for if you happen to go down to the market place as I did the other day, you will hear the most idiotic talk about not merely the rites but about the most normal features of these people's wives. The spirit is quite infectious. Everyone knows it is all lies but we sit there and laugh until we are sick and fall over backwards then become terribly gloomy until someone else starts us off again.

A liberal dose of wine helps to maintain the atmosphere. I quickly grow tired of this but the locals continue in this vein sometimes for the whole three days. More serious explanations of the women's activities involve extreme forms of sexuality, perhaps a menstruation rite and one man thought that the women were making some kind of blood sacrifice but that they were getting the victims from elsewhere. There are many plausible theories. The object of the ceremony is to increase the fertility of trees — the ostensible object at any rate. But I must not be cynical — it is merely the prevailing spirit, besides I did manage to see one part of the ritual.

There is a procession that takes place in the open air and though strictly speaking we are not admitted, there is nothing to stop us watching from a respectful distance. The women emerged from the temple in strict formation. It was all very orderly. Most wore white but some were dressed in deep red. The one in front carried a small torch.

They then took a mazy path around the fruit trees, singing a very quiet song whose words we could not make out, especially when they were circumscribing the far end of the garden. However when they approached us we did get a decent view of the parade and it became obvious that most of them were carrying some object of medium size that appeared on careful scrutiny to be a stone or wooden image of the phallus. It is amazing how a ritual becomes tiresome when one is not taking part oneself. They continued in this manner for some time, then they sat down in the centre, first placed their images by a particularly large tree, and after a while they rose and began walking again.

I got bored and started walking home. As I passed some houses near the market place I was accosted by two girls who obviously had better things to do than attend religious ceremonies. What with one thing and another I took up their offer. They had not been short of trade the last few days.

The next day I was on my way down to the market when I saw Adrian, an aquaintance from my home town, on the other side of the street, puffing and sweating his eyes swivelling in his head, obviously looking out for me. What could I do? I tried to duck down a passage but only succeeded in drawing attention to myself. He was after me in a flash. I pretended not to see him and hurried on by a roundabout way to the market on the chance that I might lose him in a crowd. Vain hope! Our chasing game lasted only a few minutes then he was upon me. Of course I had to pretend to be pleased to see him: 'What a delightful surprise' etc. He knew very well that I had attempted to escape him, but refused to confront me with the fact. He in turn pretended to be just as surprised as I was.

'Fancy meeting you here. I only came down to do some business. I am on the point of pulling off one of the biggest deals of my life; in copper. That's where the money is to be made but there is one small difficulty. On my way here, dreadful event! I was robbed by some bandits, leaving me rather short — nothing I can't easily raise once I get home of course — but inconvenient under the circumstances. But the Gods are kind. Who would have thought that here, in a foreign country I would find my dear comrade (I don't know what he means by that), Bronteas, who is known for his kindness, and for being the one man in Cyprus who is never short of ready cash. 'Here is what I propose' he continued in one breath, 'if just for once you cover my expenses here, I'll cut you in on the deal. Of course the robbers will be captured and executed, some part of my money will be recovered, and when everything is sorted out we shall both be rich. Or at least comfortable. Well, what do you say?'

I had to think quickly.

'Well, I can't promise anything, old friend, you always have exaggerated the extent of my wealth — but,' and here I pretended to consider, 'if what you say is true — and the deal does sound attractive —I'll do what I can to help you. You haven't mentioned the precise sum and I am not in the habit of carrying all my money round town with me, but here's what I'll do. If you meet me back here this afternoon I shall be able to provide you with some money and a letter of credit with my family in Carpasia. That ought to satisfy everyone.' 'Alright', said he, 'see you in the afternoon'.

Needless to say I never intended to return to the arranged place but rushed off home and packed my bags. I had prepared everything and was on the point of quitting the house when Adrian turned up. I told him he was early and asked him to wait for me round the corner. I sneaked out through the back. But I hadn't got more than a few miles out of Tamasus when I came upon him sitting by the roadside, munching cakes. There was no need for explanations. I sat down with him and shared his cakes.

We are back in Tamasus. We had progressed barely a mile beyond our last post when, I stumbled against a rock, turned my ankle and impaled myself on a particularly sharp thorn that I could not for the life of me remove. Adrian tried to help but his useless flapping succeeded only in annoying me. I wrote to my wife instructing her to send our slave Phylon. I should never have travelled without him. It makes people suspicious in the first place and besides that, I have, contrary to my expectations, found myself with an increasing amount of luggage.

There was no alternative to a very painful return to Tamasus with the dubious assistance of my friend. It had grown terribly hot; the pebbles scorched my feet and I was thirsting continually. I was afraid of fever. I always have been. I loathe the way one loses control of oneself under an attack.

Adrian has been good to me. He has brought me food, news, kept me occupied with conversation, paid the bills (with my money to be sure) and has even found me a doctor. Apparently people are gathering for another festival. I hadn't realised there would be one so soon — and among the visitors are a number of medical men.

The doctor who visited me was a most disreputable looking man, his garments soiled, his skin blotchy, his teeth bad and his smell repulsive — I had a good mind to dismiss him at once but just then I suffered a shooting pain down my leg so for a moment was incapacitated and without speech. Meanwhile he had spread his large bundle out across the floor and was examining my knee with gravity, muttering to himself in a foreign dialect.

'Can't you cure him?' asked Adrian.

That should not prove beyond my powers', answered the other. Then he selected a large white bulb. "*Sea onion*" he explained holding it up like a conjuror at a fair.

"Sacred to three gods, given to humanity by the lord of my profession, Asclepius, to keep evil spirits away from us and to reactivate dead members of our bodies. With this ordinary looking bulb I helped a seventy year old man to produce his first child . . ."

I did not believe a word he was saying, his boastful manner making it impossible for me to take him seriously.

He peeled off a segment of the bulb, asked for water and went out of the room, presumably to boil the thing for when he returned it was steaming. He slapped the soft remnant on the wound without so much as an apology (I was in agony) and fastened it tightly with a strip of cloth. Then he put his left hand on my wound and began reciting a prayer that seemed to have no end:

"Lord of wisdom, conqueror of pain, healer of wounds of the body and of the mind . . . Help break the foot of evil sin, the evil of sickness, the evil of guilt that invaded this house . . . Like this onion which I peeled and boiled on the fire, whose roots are dead and will never take hold in the ground, whose shoots will never shoot in the air, that will never make food for a god, or a king, or a man, like this onion, may the evil of pain peel off his body and may the fire of your will consume it entirely this minute . . ." etc. etc.

Once this business was over he became courteous and offered to sell us concoctions as cures for anything from the plague to impotence. A few hours later the wound opened up and the thorn oozed out along with a deal of abcess. Doctors are such odd fellows. I've never seen one that did not look utterly untrustworthy. But the pain has gone. I can walk about my room.

———————
———————

I am well now and ready to move on to **CITIUM.** The festival I mentioned took place over the last three days. It was surprisingly archaic in its pederasty and homosexual love. One of the main events was a race of naked boys. Once this used to be so in Carpasia too I believe but the custom was dropped in my grandfather Philip's time. I found it difficult to take the thing as seriously as I ought to have done — for while I think such passion natural I cannot see how Aphrodite is honoured by it —surely fecundity is the point and not amusement or gratification of everyday desires. The young men are treated quite violently and must submit to one or other of the priests under the pretence of resistance. There were some exceptionally attractive boys there.

The slave Phylon turned up yesterday much to my relief.

The road to Citium is a rough dusty path trodden out of lime stone by the feet of travellers. I wish towns who share these roads would take responsibility for their improvement and make them safe from brigands.

We walked part of the way along the dried up bed of a river. Although we could not see the sights above the river bank we enjoyed walking in the shade, on soft sand.

Once again I have arrived too early but as I am here I may as well look around. My leg is completely recovered so I am able to do as much walking as I wish. Phylon carries my belongings and Adrian intends leaving within a day or so, partly to take up my loan, partly to pursue some business interest in Carpasia.

I was surprised to find it raining when I arrived. The salt lake was still and dark and the rain punctured it everywhere with pock-marks, like beaten silver. Between the trees I could see a colony of ducks that seemed to extend for almost a mile. Then there were flamingoes that had cornered a little bay of their own. We made our way through the palms and into the town itself. The centre of Citium is on quite high ground and all the temples are situated here. The most important, of course, is the temple of Aphrodite who is called *Aphrodite – Astarte* here. The yard is always crowded with people, who come to admire a fish pond and an altar surrounded by marble walls decorated with a frieze of which *Baal* and other hereos are shown in combat with a hord of evil giants. It has great presence but it was constructed in the Phoenician fashion without any regard to the canons of proportion and harmony.

By the evening the rain had stopped and the sky was clearing,and a pleasant red glow lay over the whole area. We were lucky to find accommodation on the first floor of an inn. The ground floor is unbelievably filthy and smelly fit only for animals and the poorest travellers. Had a really fine meal prepared by the proprietor who is of Phoenician descent but who employs a number of Persians.

Space at the inn was rather limited and I had to share my room with two Syrians who were here on business. They were loud talkative men and quickly drew me into their conversation. They, along with some four others, appeared to be members of some delegation privately commissioned, and were keen on visiting the local brothel of which they had heard a great deal. It sounded an extremely low class kind of place to me but I agreed to accompany them on a visit.

It was just as I had thought, worse, and it was as well that we paid our visit after dark for I have since heard that no respectable citizen would dream of entering the place in broad daylight. At the entrance stands a statue of *Aphrodite Callipyge,* well carved and extremely enticing in the way she peeks at one over her shoulder, her hindquarters pushed out and raised in invitation. I ought to mention at this point that this brothel contained not girls but men. Inside it was dark for the torches they used were small and placed at long intervals. On closer inspection the ornaments supporting the torches turned out to be cast-iron male figures engaged in various forms of copulation. We were conducted round by a pretty boy whose long hair ws ornately curled and hung down past his shoulders. He spoke in a low whisper but would now and then erupt into coarse laughter when dwelling on some detail of the decoration. He made much of the Syrians and showed by his conversation that he was well acquainted with Syrian politics and sexual habits. However I noticed that he cast his warmest glances at me.

The murals also showed scenes of homosexual revelry whose details do not vary enough to call for a full description. Everything was

82

exaggerated of course as one would expect; a mixture of the impossibly graceful and the outrageously comical. Fat men with tiny acrobats, tiny men with gross and larded prostitutes, two muscular fellows treating the whole thing as though it were some strenuous gymnastic exercise. There were captions to many of these but I cannot remember one off hand.

Outside a warm wind had sprung up and every so often I was caught in a pleasant draught between two windows. My Syrian acquaintances were soon conducted to the rooms of their choice and I being unable to name my pleasure was left to talk with the boy. We walked around the temple together. He rather resented the low standing of his profession (the locals call them dogs) and indeed wished he had been born a woman so as to escape this odium. I consoled him by pointing out that he was very young and very beautiful and these things were not to be despised. At this he cheered up.

"We are all under the goddess's protection", he said, and we continued talking till the early hours of the morning.

I walked around the harbour. What a cosmopolitan gathering it is: the costumes alone provide a kind of gazetteer. A bright and sunny day, the sun sparkling off the water, the surf thick and very white, triremes, quinqueremes, small fishing boats, bannered masts and sails, curious prows with foreign inscriptions. On the promenade one hears many strange languages; ugly bulbous words; coughing, scratching noises; musical speeches and languages that seemed to be like ours but turn out to be indecipherable. The place is crowded too with prostitutes and cripples and packages of all sorts. I saw one man fall into the water. He must have been drowned for I did not see him surface again. No one bothered. The city has done well under the Phoenicians.

I have spent two enjoyable weeks in Citium. One of the pleasures of being here is to visit the market place and listen to strange stories brought back from far away places by sailors and merchants. I have heard of a race of one-eyed people, the Arimaspians, who live in the East, of the Lotus eaters who exist on the flowers of this water plant, and of the Albiones who have red skins and their island home is beyond the pillars of Hercules. No doubt there is an element of exaggeration in these stories but they are extremely enjoyable.

Adrian departed today in high spirits. He has joined up with a party of travellers heading East so he has some entertainment — he may even ride for they had a number of horses between them. The lovely boy is fickle.

Being tired of Citium and the weather having taken a turn for the better I decided to climb the **MOUNTAIN OF APHRODITE** * fifty stadia away and visit its famous temple. What a steep climb it is! The path is very narrow and twists and winds in the most awkward way between briars and nettles, over loose shingle and patches of slippery moss, so that one is quite exhausted by the time one reaches the top. However there are many consolations once you have begun for all along the path, by every tree, bush or outcrop you will find some sort of shrine: even rocks and the larger stones to say nothing of the shallow little caves pitting the mountainside, forming natural niches and hollows, are consecrated by priests and have altars improvised whereon are arranged the customary offerings of beans, almonds, oil or what you will, besides crudely formed wax or clay images of diseased pilgrims whose ailments are indicated by abnormalities in the relevant limbs or organs. There are some with wounds, some with swellings, several toothless. I myself stopped at one of these and moulded a likeness out of damp earth, giving it a cleft knee in memory of my recent injury. Then both Phylon and I stopped to pray; I in thanks-giving for my cure, Phylon for a sick mother; all this to the accompaniment of bird song (they sing prettily among the trees and bushes and appear very tame). Turning away I barely avoided putting my hand on a scorpion, which — the avoidance I mean not the scorpion itself — I take for a good omen, and the creature scuttled back into an overturned jar among a group of neglected statuettes.

It is a good place for prayer. Firstly, it is private: no-one can approach you without making his presence known some time before he arrives, for the ascent is steep and much noise is unavoidable; one is always breaking branches, dislodging stones or upsetting other people's offerings. Thus your pleas go unheard, irrevocable, save by divine agency. Secondly, being high above the rest of the world you can feel detached from your daily cares and appear to yourself somehow more than a man, fitter company for gods and goddesses. Thirdly, it is good to pray where many have prayed before, to feel the stones themselves sanctified by centuries of touching, or to enter a cave containing echoes of voices long dead: men of state, commoners, women and boys, old hags fatter than Silenus, probably wheezing and out of breath. It is a strange feeling. Did not Hesiod learn singing on a mountain?

Ancient coin showing the Temple of Aphrodite on Mount Eryx (Stavrovouni).

* ***Stavrovouni*** *– where Stavrovouni monastery now stands.*

Except for a few foxes and the odd hare there are no wild animals on the sacred mountain. However, we were attacked twice by savage dogs belonging to some shepherds who wander from place to place looking for new pastures for their goats. In the summer they sleep in the open air with their flocks and in winter time in some caves at the foot of the mountain. We would have been hurt badly if the dogs were not restrained by their owners.

Reaching the summit we found a group of visitors who had arrived some time ago, delegates of local farming communities, who were taking part in a water ritual, the object of which was the induction of seasonal rain. Since we had just had a day of delicious warm drizzle, it may safely be assumed that either they or a previous group had met with success. However I felt it my duty to act as the impromptu representative of my own town and joined with them in their prayers. The climax of the ceremony is spectacular and rather moving. The priest sprinkled our heads with consecrated water (this is at the altar after due offerings have been made) then we were led in procession around the temple and down to the cliff-edge, a sheer drop of frightening proportions, where the priest took what was left of the water and poured it with stylised gestures into the abyss below. We watched it fall as long as our eyes could follow it. The following day we had the interpretation of omens and detailed forecasts of rain or drought.

We have been here for close on a week now, much against our inclination, since that party of farmers that I mentioned with regard to the water ceremony was attacked and robbed by a group of bandits not a mile hence. One man returned to tell of murder and all kinds of violence, his own appearance bearing witness to the truth of his account. Apparently the farmers had hardly stepped off the mountain when they were assaulted by a group of bandits armed with spears and short-swords. One man was immediately killed, the rest taken into captivity, our fugitive managing to escape, not without conspicuous damage, after a successful struggle with two of the bandits. The priests here believe that this is a newly formed band, or perhaps one that has migrated hence from another district, for they could not recognize them from the man's description. However, they add, there is nothing unusual in this, there are frequent raids in the area, but the criminals never encroach on the mountain itself for fear of divine retribution.

This was three days ago and despite the presence of such a force there has been a steady trickle of pilgrims to the temple; individuals rather than groups. These have been people who were ignorant of the situation and one must suppose they slipped through because the robbers deemed them not worth the trouble of fleecing. Yesterday though, the remnants of another group arrived with tales of pillage and butchery so there is no reason to feel safe. All this had led to a curious situation.

The temple is so crowded that there is little room to move for none will leave now but waits here until reports arrive either of the bandits' capture or of their departure. How tiresome it is! The priests continue with their ceremonies as if nothing had happened, the gifts pile up on the altar, conversation grows stale and we are all very bored. Sometimes the priests remove some of the offerings; fruit and corn and such to the cellar, the statues to an enormous cave on the east side of the mountain. These can be very interesting I suppose, and among the bulls, monsters and human figures I came across a beautifully carved group of horned centaurs with snakes entwined about their necks. The hands of the centaurs (horse with human body, arms and head in place of its neck and head), were raised in adoration of Aphrodite who is their goddess. Even the robbers respect her it seems for there have been reports of them praying among the shrines.

We had been advised by a number of priests on which was the best route to take and they also provided us with a pair of old swords and a long curved knife, quite handsomely preserved. This descent was if anything more tortuous than our coming hence. Our legs were scratched raw by the time we were at the bottom. As this was early morning the bird song was particularly loud which helped cover up the noise we were making. Once at the foot of the mountain we were to look out for certain landmarks (unmistakeable they assured us) which would steer us clear of the area supposed to be occupied by the bandits. Apart from a few personal documents and very little money I had left all our luggage with the high priest so that in case we were spotted, we might appear less of a temptation. One moves very slowly when one is unacquainted with the terrain and our constant debates on which were the genuine landmarks and which not slowed us down still further. I don't believe we had progressed above two stadia by mid morning, yet we were hopeful that we had eluded them, for neither did we hear nor see anything remotely connected with humanity. But we were wrong. As we rounded a clump of trees we came upon a solitary horse tied up and champing the dry grass. He snorted and stamped when he caught sight of us, then two men, one of whom was leading another horse emerged from behind some bushes. We had heard them of course before they came into view and hid among the trees. From their appearance we were left in no doubt that these men were members of the gang; they were encumbered with swords. Suffice to say, they being alert and trained to open life, we were noticed and set upon with shouts loud enough to rouse every ruffian in Cyprus, so that I gave up all hope of life and determined to defend myself to the inevitable end.

Now I could not pretend that Phylon and I (however useful we were with a sword) would have been able to ovecome men like these in combat not at all suited to our more formal style, but my dreams proved good prophets. It turned out that one of the robbers was in fact already injured and badly handicapped by having his fighting hand swathed in bandages. Phylon threw his own small knife at him and I hacked off the other arm while Phylon occupied his companion, then we both set about the remaining one until we had managed to sufficiently wound him too, though powerful man as he was he inflicted a quite severe injury on Phylon in the process. But Phylon showed admirable courage and I set him on the calmer looking horse, taking the other for myself and we rode off Heaven knows where, possibly right into their arms, but in the vague direction indicated by the priests. Soon we could hear behind us the sound of horses and men and it became obvious that unless we did something unexpected we would be caught.

Now we had been riding alongside a small stream, so we quickly dismounted and set our horses off while we crossed over and stumbled away among the trees. Presumably the robbers must have ridden on for we were not followed and in time came upon an old inn, where we asked to be sheltered, for Phylon was bleeding quite badly now and it was all I could do to support him and prevent the blood leaving a clear trail for our pursuers.

We remained long enough to bandage poor Phylon's wound and to use what money we had left to buy a fresh pair of horses and employ a guide to escort us safely to Amathus.

AMATHUS is a most attractive place and I have time on my hands while Phylon recovers. Furthermore, a festival is due to be celebrated soon. First let me stress the antiquity of the city, indeed the fact impresses itself upon one at every turn; from the very trees on the adjacent hillside, the olives and carobs, whose trunks are wider than anywhere else that I had seen previously, to the buildings, gates and walls decorated with martial reliefs, the groves, the shrines and relics; all of which combine to provide an air as ancient as our legends. There is a reverse side to the coin of course: the poorer civil quarters are a disgrace, narrow dark and fouled by animals and humans alike.

To make things worse they place their sick, some with pitiful appearances, by the doorway so that passersby who had similar illnesses would give them advice. But it would not do to dwell on these things among such a wealth of grand and beautiful objects, chief among which is the temple of **Aphrodite Amathusia.** This is large enough to be seen from every part of the city, having a tower seven storeys high that represents the seven zones of the planets as well as the seven zones of the earth. I was privileged enough to be shown round this edifice by one of the attendant priests, the friendliest of men, yet not without due dignity, who obviously took great pride in his post, anticipating every question with a, "But you are about to ask . . ." and thence proceeding to tales and explanations that I wish I had the wit to remember. What did I see? Some parts I could not be shown for they were reserved for the use of the high priest, but the records library and the city archives were pointed out to me with some enthusiasm. I was impressed by the thoroughgoing symbolism of the arrangement; for everything there was a reason or precedent; no article of furniture, no image was superfluous. Perhaps it was the very wealth of coordinated detail that leaves me now a little uncertain as to the order of my impressions (for I have not the conceit to call them any more than impressions). If I may make a profane comparison I am like a man who is found laughing at some joke yet cannot for the life of him repeat the story that brought him to this state.

The priests and priestesses are provided with separate dwellings adjacent to the temple though some do actually join on to the main building. These are sumptuously furnished and decorated, unlike at Aphrodite Akrea where the priests had little more than holes to sleep in, which are themselves surrounded by smaller temples in the sacred enclosure, that are dedicated to various gods. On the ground floor of the main temple is a long hall, thickly collonaded, open to the public who may, with the assistance of the high-priest or, on occasion, one of the others, make an offering on the altar.

Here the statues of Aphrodite and Adonis, the latter portrayed as an energetic hunter, the former naked save for a necklace of green and gold stones which are not only extremely beautiful and a great focus of attention, but are also credited with marvellous (and disturbing) powers: to bestow either immortality or death. This duality, which renders the necklace a frightening fascination, is rooted in the claim that Hephaistus himself forged it as a wedding present to Harmonia, Aphrodite's daughter. Harmonia and every possessor of that necklace since has been dogged by disaster. The priests do not allow anyone to touch it.

I lodged near the port, overlooking a public square and from a window I could see the long pier stretching out into the harbour, studded with boats and packages and could hear people of many nations shouting instructions, and carriage wheels squeaking and rattling through the streets below.

But this square is dominated by an immense statue of *Hercules the Lion-Slayer,* the *Colossus of Amathus,* monstrous-headed, horned, bearded (the beard cut square and curly in the Assyrian fashion) and with long, rough hair. A lion's skin is knotted round his waist which is lean but muscular, and he holds in his hands the hind paws of a lioness whose head hangs down between his legs and whose mouth serves as a spout from which issues a powerful stream of clear water. Pigeons are sitting on his head and shoulders. Now a gull swoops down and frightens the pigeons away. It has a rude power which I find has a reassuring effect, especially at night when the sailors fall to brawling and gangs of youths pursue each other up and down the dark streets.

There is much quarreling between the inhabitants who may be divided into three parties. There are the usual Greeks and Phoenicians but more than half the population is made up of thse people whom we call proto-Cyprians, those who by tradition are thought to be descendants of the original natives of Cyprus. They are a peculiar race that do not exist anywhere else on the island, or certainly not in any recognisable community, being squat, powerful and badly proportioned: their heads and hands are far too big. They have a language of their own and are said to indulge in human sacrifice, but no doubt that is a malicious rumour, understandable in view of their haunting appearance. In times of war they tend to side with the Phoenicians and I have been made aware of some anti-Greek feeling in the city.

The oracles and soothsayers of Amathus have a scandalously poor reputation as shown by a typical example when one named Thasius, had advised the King of Egypt Busiris, to sacrifice a foreigner to Zeus in order to rid his country of a terrible plague. This was done much to Thasius' chagrin for the foreigner whom Busiris selected to be the victim was the soothsayer himself; and neither did the matter stop there, for the sacrifice having proved afficacious Busiris took it into his head to sacrifice any foreigner who set foot in his kingdom (what this did to trade I cannot

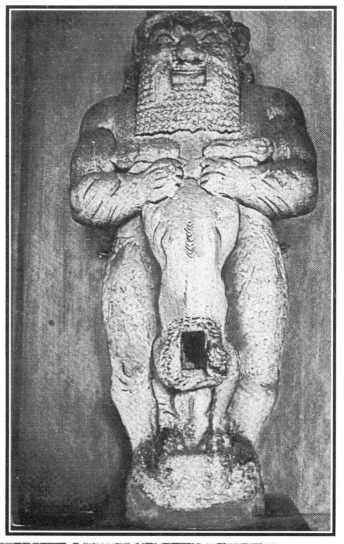

Above: Hercules, the lionslayer or as was known "The Colossus of Amathus". It dominated the main square of ancient Amathus – 6th cent. BC. (Istanbul Archaeological Museum).

Left: Akropolis of Amathus – The remains of a huge jar are to be seen. Another jar is now in the museum of Louvre.

think!). Eventually Hercules turned up and he was accorded like treatment, carried to the altar, bound hand and foot, but he had no difficulty in disentangling himself and proceeded to sacrifice Busiris and his entire family on the altar of Zeus. One may fairly describe these events as disastrous. No doubt however I shall consult my usual oracle before I quit this place.

It has been very hot here during the last week and it was difficult to summon up enthusiasm, but I joined in most of the activities of the festival of *Fruition*. One of the attractions of this festival has been a performance by a young man who convincingly imitated the cries and movements of a woman in childbirth. This relates to the myth of Theseus and Ariadne, for the people here believe that after killing the Minotaur Theseus came to Amathus with Ariadne who was pregnant and that being abandoned by him here, she died in labour. According to the legend the people cared for her while she lived and after her death identified her with Aphrodite thus instituting this festival of Fruition, in memory of her pregnancy. The idea behind the performance of the young man imitating a woman in childbirth was to divert the evil spirit that killed Ariadne and her baby from its target to kill other pregnant women in the town. At one point in the proceedings we threw the ashes of burnt meat on a tomb known as the Tomb of Aphrodite, in the same grove. It may seem queer to have a tomb for one of the immortals but the locals justify it by reference to the Ariadne incident above and in their belief that the goddess had spent some time in the land of the Dead, during her search for Adonis.

It was a very well attended festival, and the groves were crowded with pilgrims and salesmen selling all manner of things from oil and potteryware through to confections and livestock. We (for Phylon considered himself fit enough to attend) slept at night under the trees together with merchants and their wares. Given the climate it was the most sensible and refreshing thing to do: the town smelt awful.

It was not until the third day of the festival, at noon, that people began to pack up their belongings and move on. By the evening it was almost deserted save for the numerous offering arranged in the grove. All in all it was the most impressive experience of my journey so far.

Silver coin of King Lysandros of Amathus – c.375 BC.

Later I had a dreadful headache and felt nasty and sluggish. It was still scorchingly hot. I was off to Paphos. Dry bread and wine for me. I hired a mule and a muleteer who looked a perfect villain. We planned to travel this way at least as far as Curium. Phylon was fit to travel and the proxenos (consul) had supplied me with a reasonable loan.

Before I left I visited a soothsayer: terribly solemn and piercing-eyed. He contemplated me for a little while then closed his eyes and wrote out the following verses. It was his prophescy:

> *Trust to Mule and trust to Horse*
> *Heaven shall prepare your Course,*
> *Safely, pilgrim, journey on*
> *The gods shall give thee benison,*
> *Grow in wisdom and in wealth,*
> *Fear not thou the robber's stealth,*
> *Nor slave, nor corpse art like to be*
> *But shall prosper constantly.*

My poor condition and the dreadful heat of the day had obliged me to hire the mule-driver in the first place — well, we trotted along at a slow pace for some seven miles, having stopped off to bathe several times (on doctor's advice), and by sunset we had reached a milestone, surrounded by a large number of smaller stones. This formed a very large mound and it was our duty to supplement the pile with a stone each: for this acts as a sort of impromptu shrine to Hermes, protector of travellers, and also, alas, of thieves. It was interesting to note by the way that some of the larger stones had maps carved into them, complete with abbreviated place names and distances. The countryside around seemed very pleasant, closeted by vines and pomegranates, and other trees whose branches twined over our heads, so I suggested to the driver that it would make a fine camp for the night. He agreed and led us down to a delightful little crevice where flowed a thin, but quite clear brook. We cooled our wine in the stream and sat down to a satisfying meal of bread, cheese and fruit. And rather too much wine. Phylon was the first to fall asleep and I must have been next. I doubt whether the mule-driver slept at all.

The reader could perhaps supply the end of this incident without any further information from me. Let me add however that besides the money and clothes that we were carrying, I had about me certain trinkets and souvenirs of no great material value but to which I had become rather attached, to say nothing of the presents I had accumulated for friends and

92

relatives at home. When Phylon and I woke, almost simultaneously, we found that literally everything had gone; the driver the animals, our packs, our money, the necklace for my wife, the brooch for her sister, the pouches, the statuettes, the herbs, my own special effigies of Adonis and Aphrodite, and the excellent incense sold by Targon near the market place in Amathus: everything.

What was there to do? I had been stupid to trust such obvious rascal in the first place. He had left us not even a sandal to make our journey easier! We walked the remaining four miles to Curium, cursing the thief, the astrologer, ourselves, our feet, and chiefly the rough road which was covered with thorns and horrible pine-needles. Between my bad leg nd Phylon's wound it took us six hours. The city is built on a high plateau you see and in the heat it was all we could do to keep going.

CURIUM is divided into distinct parts, the Upper and the Lower City. Our first visit had necessarily to be to the proxenos representing Carpasia, a local man named Chariton with business and family connections with our town. He resides in the Upper City near the main square and he was very friendly affording us a loan without the normal precautions of 'proof and identity', for, as it turned out, he had once made a good deal with my father in the days when the old man was still sprightly. In fact he pressed us to stay as his guests, an offer which we were pleased to take up. I had not realised before what a wealthy man he was; but his mansion is magnificent with many spare rooms in a well-kept wing that has its own entrance. This meant we had absolute privacy a luxury indeed. He kept us talking late into the night and we discovered that he was quite a philanthropist and had staged five drama festivals at his own expense. The next day while exploring the town we found a column in the public square commemorating his generosity, though he had not mentioned this in his conversation. He fed and wined us so well that for the second night running we drifted off into a delicious sleep.

Both the upper and lower parts of Curium possess public squares, broad and well-kept, paved in marble. The palace of the king and the main temple of **Apollo Hylates**⋆ — the patron god of the city — are situated

⋆ *This is a very important cult in Cyprus which lasted for over 1000 years.*

in Upper Curium. The streets otherwise are dark and narrow and only men on foot are allowed through most of them in the day-time. Apparently there have been many fatal accidents involving animals and carts.

The temple is huge and comprises the treasury, the gymnasium and a free lodging house besides the usual sacred edifices. The palace I cannot speak for; it looks well enough from the outside. I was particularly impressed by three buildings: the public baths in Lower Curium which overlook the square and are fitted out with cold, hot and steam baths, two restaurants, three taverns, a games arena and a highly luxurious, though expensive, brothel; an amphitheatre at the south end of the city perched on the edge of a precipice, very pretty and dangerous; and not far from that, to the West a desolate circular platform of impressive proportions with an altar at the centre.

I went with Chariton to the platform I have just described: Already a large and festive crowd had gathered there bearing the usual religious knick-knacks. Chariton had brought another man with him and as they were chatting about business there was little chance of conversation. Then someone next to me said, 'He is coming!' and I wondered who he meant. I had quite a good view from where I stood, so craned forward to focus on a small knot of men who had entered the central space. They were several youths, three priests and a man who appeared to be bound walked among them, closely attended. For all the world it looked like a public execution or a trial of some sort. The priests stood by the altar praying and the prisoner ascended the platform. I recognised him as the mule driver, the very same scoundrel who had robbed us on the way here!

'Yes', people told me, 'it was Pandorus the murderer (twice over), thief and confidence trickster, who had been captured, tried and sentenced late last night'.

What are they going to do with him?' I asked, 'I thought this was a religious festival not a place of execution'.

'But it is a religious festival'. I was assured, 'it happens every year; a criminal bearing our sins, is sacrificed to Apollo. It is like expelling poison'.

I found it difficult to watch. After all I knew the man! What if he was the worst of villains — an execution is an execution and not an occasion for rejoicing. The man was forced to run around the perimeter of the area while the youths picked him up and ran out of the arena with him. The crowd too surged forward and there was a general rush down to the cliff-edge. Here Pandorus was swung four or five times in the air before being thrown headfirst to his death in the sea below. Thus ended our mule driver. The theft with which he was charged was not even connected with ours.

PAPHOS at last! The distance from Curium is not great but the road winds through hills and is extremely steep at times which makes for hard going. As we approached the city we were met by an ever increasing stream of pilgrims, some on foot, some on mule or horseback, converging on the city. Between Paphos and Curium there is a forest of pines where deer wander in large numbers, unafraid and unmolested —the woods of Apollo Hylates. I must mention this before passing on.

The deer are very docile. Two or three came up to us and nudged at our chests in hope of food. Of course we could not resist them. As they are under the protection of Apollo it would be sacrilege to harm them, and we took their solicitations as signs of the god's favour. At two places in the forest streams of clear water issue from the ground and here we rested and refreshed ourselves, and before leaving tossed a coin into the pool, making a wish at the same time.

A little later, at roughly the half way mark between the cities, we heard the cry of gulls and came upon a group of islands entirely composed of solid bodies of rock, on which practically every available jut and grag was occupied by some sea-bird, constantly rising and dropping with great shrieks, making it impossible for the eye to follow any single one. There were three other men standing and watching these birds, and discovering that they too were on route for Paphos we fell in with them. The border between Curium and Paphos is marked by a river that flows down from Mount Olympus. This we had to cross, then make a long and tedious ascent before we came to the gentle downhill slope that leads to the sea. This area is uninhabited but obviously skilfully irrigated and cultivated indicating that it belonged to the temple of Paphian Aphrodite.

We by-passed Old Paphos and proceeded to the port some sixty stadia distant, for this is the traditional starting point for pilgrims. What a delight this last stage of our journey was: the flat, white rooftops before us reflecting the sunlight before a clear blue sea.

We hurried towards it joyfully. Either side of the road there were sacred trees, imposing in both girth and height, and between them the tended fields stretched away in rich greens and golds. As we approached the town the road became more crowded; mules, donkeys, carts, masters and slaves blocked the road so we had to walk over the fields, but I didn't mind. At the edge of the town, quite unexpectedly, we found ourselves on the brink of a precipice, the base of which was flanked by gigantic rocks. We descended a steep path and there in front of us lay Paphos. Perhaps no place is as beautiful as a man's own home but Paphos opens out to us like a vision.

The first thing to do was to find accommodation, which was no easy task. On our way in we had seen hundreds of people wandering about with poles and makeshift tents, indeed some had already pitched them within a stone's throw of the town itself. Of course Paphos is no metropolis, and on festive occasions the local inhabitants are easily outnumbered by the visitors who come from all parts of the world. Some of the wealthy ones can afford to bribe their way into reserved rooms, others may have friends here with whom they can stay, some may be lucky enough to turn up at an inn just as others are moving out, but most people take no chances and bring camping equipment. We were of the third category.

We were just drudging dispiritedly down one of the smaller streets when a pair of drunks fell sprawling at our feet, cursing vehemently and tripping up Phylon. A man shouted disparaging comments from a doorway to the effect that he had not let his room to pigs and that such creatures would find more fitting quarters in the sty. We sized up the situation and quickly took up the vacated premises with a little bonus on top of the already rather exorbitant rent, grateful nonetheless that our long search had at last yielded some result.

However the crowding problem has another side, which as it turns out is an unusual convenience. Everyday in the appropriate season people arrive and depart, citizens of small villages, inhabitants of foreign towns, pilgrims taking a different route from the one we have chosen — there is therefore no difficulty whatever in getting a letter delivered, for hardly have you stopped to talk to someone when you discover that either he or a friend of his hails from precisely that district to which you desire a message to be sent.

The festival is not due to start for another seven days but there are plenty of things to do. The taverns are full of dancing girls and good wine and if your fancy strays to women you will find numerous houses where you will be delightfully pampered. However a little care ought to be taken, for private establishments are very expensive in season, and you could easily find yourself destitute within a few days. *The Temple girls* are less demanding financially, and leave payment to the customer's discretion, though one is expected to contribute something towards the upkeep of the temple, and the girls too must live somehow. Of course it is cheaper but there is more to it than mere cost: a temple is after all a temple and one enters in a completely different state of mind.

The Goddess had chosen the temple as her dwelling place: it is she who takes possession of a girl's body when she performs her duties willingly, and indeed I have yet to see brighter, heavier blossom than in the temple gardens of Paphos.

Another way of filling in the time is to hire a guide to take you around the town. They tend to be garrulous in the extreme and either bore you with recitations of inaccurate history or, if they think you gullible enough, make up facts with an abandon usually reserved for tumblers and dancing girls of the most audacious sort. Battles, miracles, murders are supposed to have taken place at every street corner. The guides are expensive but if you are lucky you might find a genuine and entertaining man who will make your stay more interesting than it otherwise might have been.

Since arriving here I have had the time to inquire about alternative arrangements for accommodation. There is a temporary shelter provided by the city authorities in a vacant field. This is far from comfortable and is chiefly a desperate measure, at least for people of some substance: the poor of course have no choice. Then there are various clubs that one may 'join' for a price that provide a floor to sleep on and twenty people to share it with; actors, soldiers, merchants, whatever you declare yourself to be. These are more expensive but hardly more desirable, for they are ideal haunting grounds for thieves.

As I have always said, one needs luck. My landlady is called Tyrranis, a name that fits her well. We managed to obtain the vacant room from her only after a substantial deposit, and that on the excuse that the room had in fact been reserved for a couple of other gentlemen, but that we looked very respectable, as if we could afford a poor woman some security, for after all there were so many shifty characters about who would take advantage of her generosity, and argue about the reasonable rent which was really a piffling sum considering the cleanliness and convenient siting of her house. The formalities of sale-talk are beyond me, for it must have been quite obvious to her that we would take the room at almost any price, but it was impossible to stop her. She would on no account accept foreign money.

Would we please go down to the port where we would find the local bankers at their tables, and seek out one Hereidos, a particular friend of hers who would charge us only 5% rather than the customary 6% for changing our currency.

I sent Phylon down to do this. While he was away she plied me with offers of girls and boys at cut-throat prices, but I kept assuring her, with moderate success, that the only thing I was presently interested in was a place to lay my head, a privilege for which she could consider herself as good as paid. To do her justice the house is comparatively clean but she must make a fortune, for it is a large house and most of the guests, including ourselves sleep above the stables of which there are ten, arranged in a semi-circle round the yard. We reach our room by way of a long balcony that runs the length of the compound, a set of stairs at either end. My room is not intended for 'stay-at-home' guests: its furniture consists of a solitary bed.

The social life of the city revolves round clubs and every person in the area belongs to one or other of them. They remain open day and night and are full of conversation; gossip, information, abstract argument, trade deals; off season they are really professional associations but boundaries blur at this time. Their chosen representatives sit on the City Council, which in turn, advises the King. Actors, potters, builders, even slaves have their appropriate clubs — Phylon has in fact joined this last and has made some useful contacts — but there are also those with a merely social function where common attitudes rather than common livelihoods form the basis.

There is a Literary Association, a Ladies Circle, a travellers club, and anyone may join these for an annual subscription which covers funeral expenses and a memorial tablet when a member dies. Most of the clubs maintain their own burial chamber — quite palatial affairs some of them —where members are interred. One can trace back generations of builders and fish-merchants in gaunt subterranean halls, guarded by Doric columns, accessible through silent quadrangles. The oldest tombs belong to the Phoenicians of the city who started the custom.

Phylon attended a festival called **Hierodouli,** which is celebrated by the local slaves. He had heard about it down at his club and described the proposed proceedings with great enthusiasm so that in all fairness I felt it would be wrong of me to refuse him permission. He really is a very good man, the best slave I have ever had, and highly intelligent.

98

The Hierodouli, he explained, always takes place a week before the Aphrodisia proper, and is a few days in preparation. Branches of the myrtle tree are used to build huts, and inside these huts are placed the usual stone and wax figures of the goddess, upon a bed of soft grass or other greenery. Honours are paid to an ivory statue of Aphrodite, which is credited with magical powers and has symbolic associations with the story of Myrrha and her transformation, as well as with Pygmalion's statue, that lived and walked by the goddess's aid. The slaves garland themselves with flowers and take their places in the huts trusting that the ritual would benefit their powers of procreation. Many have visions or go into trances. They say that apparitions of their free ancestors and their far away countries sometimes appear. As for the efficacy of the rites, Phylon is childless, so I earnestly join in his prayer.

Paphos possesses only one amphitheatre but it can seat up to 30,000 people, today, being the first day of the Festival Plays, all the seats were taken. During the festival there are continuous performances everyday from early afternoon to late in the evening, and a panel of judges award prizes to the finest authors and actors of each particular day. On the evidence of this afternoon's entertainment I would say the standard falls somewhat short of the best, but in their rude simplicity the plays can be very moving if a little declamatory. Mostly these are tragedies; chance and human folly are the directing forces, few however are moral or speculative in any challenging way: The statement is made, the consequences follow and one does not question the characters' motives or the assumptions of the plot.

Some have happy endings like the prize winning performance I attended. It was called CINYRAS and showed how the Paphian Priest-King dealt quite successfully with conflicting moral and religious principles at the time of the Trojan War. The plot went as follows:

> Ulysses arrives at Paphos with a Greek force and requests Cinyras's aid in the proposed Trojan expedition. Cinyras cannot refuse because the Greek forces are overwhelming, so swears to contribute forty ships. The Greeks leave and Cinyras is left to ponder on his dire situation, for as High Priest of Aphrodite he may not provide forces for the destruction of Troy, the side favoured by the Goddess, nor, on the other hand may he break his solemn promise for fear of devine vengeance. Being a pragmatist he hits upon the ingenious solution of sending but one ship, with thirty-nine small scale models on board. This is despatched to Agamemnon, the commander in chief of the

Above: "Lady at the Window" – A prostitute/priestess of Aphrodite with her characteristic headscape.
Left: Priest of Aphrodite with Dove – probably a statue of King Cinyras.
Right: "Goddess" figure from Paleapaphos area (Cyprus Museum).
Below: Ancient coin showing the Temple of Aphrodite at Paphos.

Greek forces, thus absolving himself of his oath, while avoiding the offence to Aphrodite. As a palliative he encloses a magnificent breast-plate for Agamemnon to wear — the very breast-plate described by Homer in the Iliad.

The moral? In this world you must have your wits about you!

How crowded Paphos has become! I thought the place was more than full when I first arrived but now there is barely room to move. Greeks, Egyptians, Persians, Ethiopians, jostle in the streets and all I hear are foreign voices and the cries of tradesmen. Some brothels are shutting their doors and allowing in only regulars, or those who look particularly rich or important. The temples are popular of course as is the museum. I was there this morning but could hardly see the exhibits. It is housed within the main temple enclosure and contains many objects of veneration: sculptures of gods and heroes, paintings, armour, spoils of war and other historical fragments. What do I recall? There was Pygmalion's Galatea statue, the hide and tusks of the boar that killed Adonis, and the robe and lyre of Cinyras, the lyre with which he outplayed Apollo in a contest. The sword of Teucer is also here among other Homeric relics; the golden apple with which Paris, by awarding it to Aphrodite rather than Athene or Hera, effectively commenced the Trojan War, and the box given by Phylis to her unfaithful husband Demophon which drove him mad as soon as he opened it. All these things are here arranged in hierarchies of local interest: I caught a glimpse of most of them . . .

The **Aphrodisia** begins on the sea front — the very place where Aphrodite first touched land, marked now by her favourite shrine: two large conical stones propped against each other, forming an arch surmounted by a carved dove, and sheltering a statue of the goddess gazing out over the sea. This statue set on a plinth while, on either side of the arch stands a column, heavy footed, like sentinels in pairs. The arch I must explain is no artifice but a natural wonder such as nature often throws together by chance or hidden design (like the tree outside Carpasia in the shape of an old woman with sagging breasts) and the image looks more perfect within it than it might have in a more ordered structure — she looks the goddess herself.

First came the Oiling. We stood in prayer, while a Priestess rubbed the statue all over with fine oil, then she wiped it off. The virgins came forward, young girls just into puberty, and washed their naked bodies in the waves. Then they danced a short time caressing all the while an effigy of the goddess, which they passed among themselves. The nature of this dance is purely sensual and provides initiation into the arts of seduction and sensual life. The priest signals the end of the dance with a gesture to welcome the arrival of Autumn, the time for the gathering of fruits, and the girls disperse, seeking lovers among the crowd.

Then the priest led us to the main temple, a long walk through the extensive Sacred Gardens. The path before and after this was lined by street-vendors selling incense and small effigies of the goddess. They did a roaring trade and on the way up I saw several vacated stalls, presumably because their occupants had sold out all their stock. Yet often just as one man would be packing up, a second would arrive with a fresh lot to take over his pitch. I bought some incense and a couple of figurines.

As soon as we arrived at the temple we were offered refreshments and invited to look around. I knew something of its history already, having paid close attention to a series of paintings in the museum which showed the building at different stages. At one time it used to be a modest structure, neither big nor particularly ornate, built by King Cinyras on the site of an older temple which had been dedicated to a goddess known as the *Great Mother,* but as its fame grew and spread over the whole world, and the pilgrims gathered with their wealth and piety to consult the resident oracle, it increased in size and splendour until few temples in the world could vie with it. Thus it is today. In front of the great gate (a little away removed from it) stand two pylons wreathed in pomegranates and surmounted by doves. Behind these a line of rose bushes defines a semi-circular enclosure at the centre of which is an altar. The gate itself is decorated with reliefs of soldiers, hunters and priests, and two tall towers stand either side of it joined together at three quarters of their height by three adjoining chambers with windows. On the flat roof of the chambers are displayed the emblems of Aphrodite — the crescent moon and a star. Past the gate a covered collonade extends to a black statue of the goddess, which is itself exposed to the weather, though tradition proclaims that no rain has ever fallen on it. The outside walls of the temple are built of bricks and the roofs made of clay. The sacred enclosure is large and contains the main temple, numerous sacred trees and the living quarters of its various officials, both priests and priestesses. There is a treasury, a storehouse of all the marvellous donations made by wealthier visitors and also of various records and spoils of war in an underground chamber.

But I must not forget a more natural yet no less special attraction,

Aphrodite's harbingers, the sacred doves that depart in the ealy summer but always reappear in time for the great festival. These doves are reputed to accompany the goddess on her annual visit to Lybia: their safe return is a sign of Aphrodite's presence in Paphos — also of her approval and participation.

So much for the temple. The next three days were taken up by sacrifices, prayers, singing and dancing competitions, readings of poetry, athletics, love feasts in the woods around the temple — in fact such a turmoil of activity that I cannot claim to have it properly in perspective.

The sacrifices are the most impressive: these take place throughout the day, beginning in the morning, at first light. Of course we had all seen sacrifices before but never such pomp, precision or significance.

As a member of the Actors Club I was entitled to participate in any of the performing arts, though of course this was not expected of one who had only the previous week joined and was likely to leave within the following week. I did perform however and this is how it came about.

A day before the Aphrodisia got under way I visited the club and was drawn into a conversation concerning the relative merits of various metrical schemes in religious poetry and I found myself taking the side of one of the local experts who was both actor and poet. We agreed on everything so wholeheartedly that we left the company and decided to toast each other's health the rest of the evening. It turned out that he was indeed to read one of his latest works, specially composed for the Aphrodisia, and he recited it to me, some three or four times with different intonations, asking my opinion on the effectiveness of each. We tried it one way then the other, analysed it, declaimed it, whispered it, until I knew it almost as well as he did himself. We drank until late into the night then went home our different ways.

The following morning a boy tapped at my door with a message from my new friend that I was to follow his son round to the house as urgently as possible. I did so and it turned out that the poet on his way home last night had fallen down and broken some ribs, and was now confined to his room. Would I be kind enough, he beseeched me, to learn his verses and perform them in his place the day after the next? We were so much in sympathy, he assured me that I was certain to give a moving performance and win a prize. So I became the focus of attention in the temple grounds one night. It is a pity to ruin such a happy story by admitting that I won no prize and thus disappointed my friend, but honesty compels me to own that I shall never rival the professional readers in dramatic and visual presentation (though I have a sneaking conviction that my performance was more truly felt and correctly interpreted than most of the winning ones). It was very exciting nevertheless and perhaps now I shall have alternative occupation in my old age.

There is so much to say about the Aphrodisia that I cannot include everything. There is so much free food that I have doubts whether I will be recognized when I get home: my belly is swollen and my cheeks are red, unusual sights!

THE APHRODISIA is the central event at this time, but coincident with and relating obliquely to it are the Mysteries of the Cinyraids.

I was unable to attend the secret rites, though I had plenty of opportunity to witness the four days of preparation and trial that any would-be initiate must undergo: many fall by the wayside here and one may be excluded for any defect in character, which means of course that most people with a grain of conscience will think twice about attempting it. Mind you I have seen the unceremonious dismissal of a fellow who was discovered to have a criminal record. Really this is for higher adepts, those who will enter into close and mysterious communication with the Goddess.

Suitable persons of both sexes and all ages can be initiated and those who succeed to go through the course are protected by Aphrodite in life and beyond the grave. The rites are a combination of punishment for the flesh and excitement for the spirit.

On **the first day** there is a fixed rota of strenuous physical competitions, running, wrestling and gymnastics. Not all candidates are equally fit and it is a pathetic though not uncommon sight to see some ludicrous figure attempt headstands, somersaults and such.

The second day is devoted mainly to sea-bathing, but I missed this owing to other commitments.

The third day calls for less exertion, and consists of devotional exercises and oblation chiefly the ceremonial offering of wine, fruit and flowers. There were half the

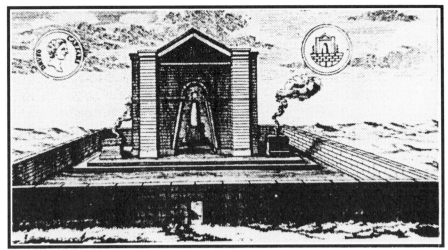

Above: Reconstruction of the Sanctuary of Aphrodite (J.B. Fischer von Erlach).
Left: The Conical Stone – symbol of the Goddess of Love (Kouklia Museum).
Below: Two Coins showing the Temple of Aphrodite.

The remains of the once full of life and mysteries Temple of Aphrodite at Kouklia.

105

candidates left by this stage. Those who had survived so far then spent the last day fasting and in constant prayer which eliminated a few more. The hardy few then paid the necessary fee to the high priest and received in return a lump of salt and a stone phallus (salt being emblematic of the sea, Aphrodite's birthplace, and the phallus of creativity). Thus abandoning the life of the senses, as symbolized by the money, and assuming a more spiritual existence. Even so, before being admitted into the temple the novices are made to take another view of purity and must bathe in holy water. And these are only the preliminary stages — the initiation now begins in earnest.

Needless to say I would know nothing of the following had it not been for information given to me by an acquaintance who had got so far once but was terribly disappointed to succumb to a fever which prevented him from completing the course.

According to him the *first advanced stage* is the reading of the mysteries by a priest. Questions are then asked in a cryptic form and these had to be correctly answered. My acquaintance did so but refuses to elaborate on the nature of the mysteries or of the questions because to do so he ran the risk of bringing upon his head divine vengeance. I naturally did not press him.

Next they are offered pancakes and honey and are declared mystics. I almost forgot to add that they wear certain garments during this last ceremony which acquire magical powers to cure illness and repel evil and for this reason they are sought after.

It was at this point that my informant contracted fever. He hung on desperately for the first day of the *second stage* but will say very little about it save that it lasted two days and he took part in some unspecified rituals connected with the myth of Adonis. One can easily imagine that this part of the ceremony was to initiate the mystics to the promise of a union with the goddess and the possibility of eternal bliss. For Adonis was the forerunner of all mystics who proved that for those favoured by the gods there was life and love after death.

Neither he, nor anyone else knows anything of the *third and final stage* which takes place in the bed chamber of Aphrodite in the temple, but men of course make vulgar guesses at obscene and sadistic forms. It may safely be assumed that the experiences are ecstatic, one theory being that emblems of the goddess are employed in some way. One man asserts that an obelisk is used as well as the sacred doves.

I have decided to stay in Paphos for a while. In a few weeks time most of the foreign pilgrims will have gone and I will be able to wander round town at a leisurely pace. The sea will be choppy next month, so they must go soon. Besides, then I will be able to seek fresh accommodation: this Tyrranis woman is quite unbearable. If it's not, 'Make sure your feet are clean before treading on my floor!' it is 'Let me introduce you to my cousin. She is a virgin, young, but so clever, you would not believe the things she can do!' Indeed she is right. I cannot believe what she says at the best of times.

But it is fruitless complaining — I shall continue dreaming of a decent comfortable room in civilised company. I shall probably be home before the Adonia if all goes well.

Gradually the fact dawns on me that I shall soon be home. I have not mentioned the times when I have felt utterly wretched and homesick. But it is always sad to come to the end of something, especially of a project one has been planning for years. I shall miss the element of risk, that pleasantly intoxicating feeling of having neither duty nor home to draw me into regular ways.

During the last few weeks of my stay in Paphos I managed to find new lodgings but only after a very nasty scene with the inn-keeper Tyrranis, who presented me with a vastly inflated bill, and tried to conjole me into staying according to the rules of some contract which I had never set eyes on. What screaming there was and what stabbing of fingers! Phylon and I eventually just pushed her out of the way and left her threatening dire forms of vengeance. I hope never to meet such a monster again.

But the rest of the time was most restful: slowly the town emptied, and the pace of life slowed down to a gentle stroll. Phylon and I frequented our respective clubs and my poet friend recovered and forgave me for letting him down in the competition. We went drinking and walking along the sea, paid regular visits to the temple and the museum and I struck up a relationship with our new landlord who was quite glad to let a vacant room. And so the days drifted on and grew colder and I almost forgot the purpose of my visit until one day it came to me that the **Marium Adonia** was almost on us. We sadly packed and bid farewell to all our recent acquaintances, promising to return, to maintain contact and so forth, and left. I don't know when I will return for one cannot do this sort of thing regularly, but perhaps, having made some useful contacts here, I will have a pretext.

After Paphos, **MARIUM** seems rather insignificant, and I cannot bring myself to give a detailed description of its ordinary streets, its humble temples and the strange religious habits of its inhabitants who eat pork and burn live doves in an oven as sacrifice to Aphrodite. I have been here for a week now and I am increasingly thinking of my homeward journey. Often during the last few days my thoughts have returned to Paphos, and I have been strongly tempted to retrace my steps and spend a few more weeks there. But these things are impossible: one can no more cast off the ties of normal life than the colour of one's hair. However I shall certainly make a point of visiting Paphos again. I have a little money in my purse, which will do to pay off my landlord and buy some food for the return journey.

Above: King Cinyras and a band of followers sailed to Cyprus and founded Paphos.
Left: A Tomb of Adonis; such tombs existed in many towns of Cyprus where the young god was worshipped.

108

Chapter Four

SURVIVING INFLUENCES OF THE CULT OF APHRODITE IN CYPRUS

T he worship of Aphrodite and other nature divinities has never ceased to be part of the religion of the Cypriot people. The Orthodox Church, unable to eradicate the deep rooted beliefs and prejudices of a people used to worshipping many gods, tried to incorporate some of these into Christian practice. Crucifixes and emblems of saints are still placed on the trunks of sacred trees and inside sacred caves, and many springs and wells are believed to produce holy water which have miraculous properties. This does not mean that Cypriot Christianity is based on pagan religion, it merely suggests that certain forms of worship as well as a number of images and symbols have been borrowed from an earlier tradition and are made to serve the new faith. There is, after all, great similarity between some old and some new beliefs, for example, between the belief of ancient polytheism which holds that individual spirits inhabit all things, and the Christian belief that the spirit of God resides in all things.

Some trees on the mountain of Stavrovouni are held to be sacred, notably an old pine tree which has assumed a biomorphic aspect and appears to be kneeling as though at prayer. The tree has a cross nailed to its bent trunk and is offered food, drinks and prayers by pilgrims who believe that it has bent over in reverence of St Helena as she passed, on her way to build the famous monastery at the summit of the mountain. Other people believe that the pine was originally exceedingly proud and had ignored the saint, who then retaliated by blasting it with a thunderbolt which caused it to repent and kneel. This kind of free-worship survives in many parts of Cyprus. Miraculous trees which are believed to cure diseases are usually found near tombs of saints and are always covered with rags of clothing and human hair hung by devotees on their branches. The most famous of these sacred trees is the *Mastic* tree of **St Solomoni** in Kato Paphos. It grows out of the tomb in which the saint and her seven children were buried alive. Visitors dedicate to it their handkerchiefs and pieces of their clothing which hang on its branches like flags. The maids of Paphos collect the gum of the sacred tree and chew it to acquire sweet and aromatic breath.

Olive trees are as sacred to the modern Cypriot peasant as Myrtle trees were to his ancestors. They believe that the first olive tree grew out of Adam's grave which is a variation of the myth of Myrha's transformation into the Myrtle. People who sleep under an Olive tree enjoy pleasant dreams and to dream of an Olive tree is a good omen that signifies a speedy and happy marriage. The oil of the olive is believed to have medicinal properties and is freely rubbed on the bodies of sick people to ease pain. It is particularly effective against ear ache when warmed in a teaspoon over a candle and poured in the affected ear. Olive oil is as indispensable to Orthodox Christian rituals as the resin of the Myrtle was necessary to Adonian rites. It is used to annoint newly baptist babies and the bodies of the dead before burial.

The Cypriots celebrate an *Olive Sunday* during which branches of the Olive tree are taken into churches to be consecrated for use as incense. These branches remain in the church for forty days and are taken home by their owners who burn them in portable incense burners, to fend off the evil eye. It is believed that witches avoid entering a house where a blessed olive branch is kept and for this reason these are hung above doorways of living rooms and stables. On New Year's Day, fresh leaves of the olive tree are thrown onto wood fires by girls and boys who at the same time sing a three verse poem in which they entreat St Basil to tell them whether or not their sweethearts are true. The fresh leaves usually leap out of the fire and the length of the leap indicates the depth of a lover's feeling. If the leaf jumps three times it means marriage in the near future but if it burns without movement it means celibacy.

Many of the flowers which ancient Cypriots used to dedicate to Aphrodite are now associated with the **Virgin Mary.** Several of them such as the Lithospermon and the Satyrium go under the name *Tears of Virgin Mary* because, after the death of Jesus, it is beleved that the heartbroken Mother wandered about the countryside in a crazed condition looking for her son, much as Aphrodite looked for the dead Adonis. White ·flowers grew out of her tears and red ones out of the blood of Jesus. Bion's epitaph for Adonis seems to fit the death of Christ very well:

> *"Where streams his blood, there blushing springs the rose*
> *And where a tear has dropped, a wind-flower blows."*

The Myrtle tree of course has not been entirely replaced by the Olive for it is still used in churches at festival times, and the coaches taking villagers to religious festivals are always decorated with its branches.

The rose of Aphrodite is still a symbol of beauty and love in Cyprus, as it is in many other countries, the half-opened bud representing the beginning of romantic feeling and the fully blown flower the maturity of perfect love. The apple of Aphrodite, and sometimes her pomegranate, are thought to be the fruit of the tree of knowledge which tempted Eve. Basil the herb of Ares, has something of paradoxical reputation in modern Cyprus. It is regularly introduced into churches, it is cultivated more or less in every village yard, and is dear to women and lovers; a man who accepts a branch of the scented herb from a woman will fall in love with her. Yet on the other hand it is considered as an emblem of hatred and death. These contradictory views of the Basil relate to Are's double role, as lover of Aphrodite and the killer of Adonis.

The *Asphodel* which ancient Greek Cypriots associated with the underworld is disliked by modern Cypriots in spite of its obvious beauty. It is still considered to be the plant of the dead and is an emblem of grief.

Some current ideas about death and the underworld in Cyprus have their roots in the religion of ancient Greece and Rome. Cemeteries are hallowed places dominated by the mournful Cypress, the tree of Pluto. Even the habit of feeding the dead survives to a degree. In some villages, instead of placing a cross at the head of a grave, they prefer an open-ended ceramic beehive in which they place *collyva*, a mixture of boiled corn, sugar and pomegranate seeds. Collyva are also distributed among the congregation at the end of special church services for the dead and are eaten in the church yard, which in many cases also serves as a graveyard. This custom is not unlike the picnics ancient people had on the graves of their dead relatives.

The ferryman of the Styx is still called **Charon** and continued to convey the souls of the dead to the Underworld. He shares responsibilities with **Archangel Michael** (*who has replaced Hermes as the messenger of God*) but unlike Michael, Charon is not represented in church ikonography. In folk songs he is usually described as *"black"* and *"heartless"*, though in some folk stories he is represented as a kindly old man who executes God's will and helps deserving people to acquire wealth and secure the future of their unmarried daughters before he gathers their souls. His mother lives with him in the kingdom of the dead and advises him to keep away from children but, as we know, there is no flexibility in his duties. On one occasion he forgot himself and engaged in a three day wrestling match with the Cypriot hero **Degenis.** When he was reminded by angels of his errand he turned himself into an eagle, sat on the head of his powerful opponent and plucked his soul out.

The name of **Hades** is still remembered but instead of being the King of the Underworld, it is a name-place now. It is believed that all souls of the dead go to Hades, which is a gloomy and dark place, but is neither hell nor paradise. It seems that souls stay there until they are judged, and then are escorted either to Paradise or to Hell.

The bodies of the dead are washed before burial in the custom of ancient Greece. As we know from Sophocles, Antigone washed the bodies of her dead mother, father and brother with her own hands.

Cypriot people will go to any length to avoid the hostility of the dead who may have influence with the spirits of the underworld or may have supernatural powers of their own. For this reason they pay homage to all the dead, including their dead enemies. When a funeral procession goes by, people stand up, take their hats off and cross themselves. When the name of a dead person is mentioned it is accompanied by the phrase *"God bless him!"* Other funeral practices inherited from the pagan past include the hysterical wailing, the decoration of graves with flowers and the lighting of candles.

Throughout the ages man has felt threatened by malevolent spirits. As a protection for himself, his family and his property against these invisible enemies with their magical powers he has used a variety of amulets which he fastened on his body or displayed on prized possessions. Man believes that even gods, heroes and devils have used amulets in their struggles against each other because they too depended on magic for their achievements. As we know from the Creation Epic of the Babylonians, the champion of the gods Marduk set out to fight the rebellious Kingu carrying an amulet in the form of an eye between his lips. After defeating Kingu, Marduk took from him the Tablet of Destinies (another amulet) which had been the source of his powers and subseqeuntly fastened it on his own chest. In Christian mythology when Satan rebelled against God the army of angels managed to defeat him by means of a cross on which were written the names of the Father, the Son and the Holy Spirit. Satan and his followers who could not face the luminous cross and its great power, turned their backs on it, their knees weakened, and the angels of the Almighty were able to hurl them down into the abyss of hell.

Early Christian fathers tried to discourage the use of amulets because of their association with black magic but their efforts had no effect. Amulets are still worn by men and women all over Cyprus and some of

Katholiki church also known as "Our Lady Galatariotissa, next to the ruins of the ancient Temple at Kouklia.

Left: The entrance to Ayia Solomoni Catacomb – Paphos.

Below: Ayios Agapitikos hermitage (St. Eros) – Paphos.

these, shaped like cats eyes and found by farmers while tilling their land, are extremely ancient. But the most popular amulets in Cyprus today are gold and silver crosses produced by jewellers all over the island. Their potency as a source of magical power is recognised even by non Christian Cypriots who use the cross as a weapon against troublesome spirits.

In ancient times amulets were designed and produced in specialised workshops like the one at Lemba which produced the famous cruciform figurines worn by women as protection against the evil eye. They were carved out of stones believed to have inherent powers to prevent disease, to cure sterility and reduce menstruation. An interesting aspect of these early amulets, dating back to the chalcolithic period, is that they have the shape of crosses and in this respect they resemble the more recent Christian amulets. Most of them represent the figure of a woman in childbirth with her arms outstretched to form a cross with the body; the outstretched arms of some of these curious figurines read like male figures. The neck and head in all of them is distorted to assume the look of erect phalluses. The symbolism of these skilful and highly sophisticated images is a complicated one but the main point in them is to show that the miracle of life begins at the point where opposite elements, such as the male and female, meet and harmonise.

The cross amulet of the Christians, like the phallic images of ancient pagans, is a powerful protection against evil spirits, and in common with pagan equivalent, is also connected with the idea of creative opposites. But in this instance the opposites do not harmonise, rather they remained in destructive conflict until a new and more powerful force was born. In other words, the cross as an instrument of death has destroyed Christ in his human form but out of this defeat and humiliation comes the resurrection and the promise of eternal life. The cross, like the boar that killed Adonis, has become an object of veneration because of its predestined role in the miracle of resurrection.

Those mythical creatures that used to haunt the Cypriot countryside in Greco-Roman times continue to exist in the popular imagination. Indeed there is no spring, river, or landmark with unusual features without its guardian spirit. The fawns, satyrs and nereids of old times are now separated into two categories, the **"Zodia"** which have a zoomorphic nature and guard streams, springs and water wells, and the **"Stihia"** (spirits) which are ghostlike, inhabit woods and bushlands, and are visible to a few hypersensitive people only. These creatures are playful and quite harmless but they are feared in Cyprus because of their monstrous

114

appearance and their habit to appear from nowhere, like Pan used to do in the old days, to frighten people and their animals.

The most fearful of the zoomorphic spirits take the shape of boars and swine; they usually have twenty piglets and are armed with two sharp tusks. But in spite of their reputation for extreme cruelty, the worst they have ever done was to chase individuals for a short distance and then return to their watery den. The ghostly "Stihia" usually take a priapic faun-like appearance and can be a prolonged nuisance to lone travellers with a sensitive nature. Their annoying trick is to stand in one's way and prevent one going forward in any direction. A protection against them has been to make the sign of the cross which, usually makes them disappear but on occasions one has to shout obscenities at them before they depart.

From these examples it is clear that Cypriots commonly believe in the existence of many spirits in nature and in the miraculous powers of some objects. In another subject we have mentioned how the black stone of the goddess, built into the wall of a church, was visited by childless women who believed in its powers to cure sterility. There are other examples of this kind of folk custom where certain church ikons are venerated for similar reasons. In the district of Paphos there exist the ruins of an orthodox church dedicated to **Our Lady Aphroditissa** (*The Venus Mary*). **Our Lady Galatariotissa** is another church in the same district whose name probably derives from Galatea, the wife of Pygmalion. The Virgin Mary represented in this church has the power to cure all mothers who have lost their ability to produce milk for their babies. In another church, at Yeroskipos village, is an ikon of *"Our Lady of the Sweet Kisses"*.

Even the girdle of Aphrodite, famous for its power to enslave the hearts of men, is still in existence and in use in the monastery of Trooditissa: it is now called the belt of the *Blessed Virgin Mary* and is lent out to Christian ladies who wish to become pregnant. The monastery of Khrysorroyiatissa, on the same mountain range, when translated freely means *Our Lady of the Golden Breasts,* although the church authorities claim that the name derives from the hill on which it stands and simply looks like a female breast and has nothing to do with Aphrodite. Visitors to both these monasteries, who might desire a cure, offer to the Queen of Heaven wax models showing the afflicted part of the body in similar fashion to the way their sick ancestors did when visiting the temple of Aphrodite. Engaged couples, and lovers in general, visit St George of the Island, a saint who is particularly understanding of their problems. Young men go to him to pray that they may be given the girl of their choice. His church is in the district of Paphos overlooking the seashore, and opposite a small uninhabited island. Here the ikon represents St. George of the Island as a handsome, virile youth, like Adonis.

In the village of Kato Paphos there are two shrines belonging to Aphrodite's old companions Eros and Anteros who have now become **St. Eros** and **St. Anteros.** Their shrines are carved into rocks and both contain altars on which visitors light candles or dedicate strips of their clothing. The functions of the two saints are similar to those of their ancient counterparts, namely that one creates feelings of love and the other either punishes those who fail to respond to love or terminates romantic associations he considers to be improper. There are two ways to procure the assistance of these two saints — one either donates to them a piece of clothing belonging to the person whose affections one wishes to influence or one takes a sample of soil from the shrine and scatters it over the person one loves. The saints seem to use these items to identify their target. There is an element of risk involved in using this venue to gain somebody's affection, for few people can now tell with certainty which shrine belongs to which saint, and as we know the two divinities performed opposite functions. While examining these shrines, I was approached by an old lady and was advised by her to return to the spot at sunset and to stand at the correct distance from the rocks. I was now to watch for the appearance of a pig-like shadow on one of the shrines which belonging to St. Anteros, would help identify the respective shrines.

The pig is of course connected with the cult of Aphrodite. It was the Boar that killed Adonis, and even now, no pork is eaten at wedding feasts for fear that the bride might become a widow. These wedding feasts last for three days, like the Aphrodisia festival celebrating the union of the goddess with her lover Adonis. After the church ceremony it is customary in some villages to offer the bridegroom a pomegranate (sacred to Aphrodite) which he then cracks on the door of the wedding chamber. A similar event involving the pomegranate takes place at moslem Turkish Cypriot weddings. In other villages the bridegroom is required to kill a cockerel (sacred to Eros) and spray the blood onto the doorstop of the wedding chamber. Both events are types of sacrifice belonging more to ancient traditions than Christian culture. But there are also great differences in wedding habits of ancient and modern Cyprus, the most striking of which is the claim of modern Cypriots that the ultimate satisfaction is the deflowering of a virgin and the insistence that their wives be virgins on their wedding day. In earlier centuries (attitudes are nowadays changing), this ambivalent attitude has had some tragic results, leading in extreme cases to murder.

One of the best known festivals in Cyprus takes place on Whit-Sunday and its origin seems to be rooted in the **Aphrodisia.** This is held in all coastal towns and includes competitions of song, dance and swimming. On the calendar of the Orthodox Church it is marked down as the *Festival of Deluge* but there is no doubt that the Cypriots who flock to the beaches to splash each other with water are celebrating the birth of Aphrodite rather than a Biblical event.

Many other Christian festivals owe their origin or are heavily influenced by pagan traditions. Few historians today will argue against the view that the festival of Christmas was borrowed from the Roman religion and has its origin in the celebration of the winter Solstice. The first Christmas celebration sanctioned by the church took place in the 5th century A.D.

Sir James George Frazer in *'The Golden Bough'* quotes an early Christian writer on the subject as follows:

> "It was the custom of the heathen to celebrate on the twenty-fifth of December the birthday of the sun, at which they kindled lights in token of festivity. In these solemnities and festivities the Christians also took part. Accordingly, when the doctors of the Church perceived that the Christians had a leaning to this festival, they took counsel and resolved that the true Nativity should be solemnised on that day . . . "

Celebrations on 25 December were held throughout the Middle East. The Egyptians held midnight services in their temples at the end of which they cried *"The Virgin has given birth, the light begins to wax"*. The Cypriots, like the Egyptians and other Middle Eastern people believed that the Sun was born from a goddess called **Heavenly Virgin,** which was one of the titles of Aphrodite — Astarte, and during the celebrations they exhibited the image of an infant in the same way that many Christian churches do at Christmas today. Epiphanius, the great bishop of Cyprus, tells us that the Saracens also held a feast in honour of Aphrodite on 25 December.

But the greatest festival on the church calendar is Easter, and here one may find further correspondence between the old Adonian rites and the present Christian form. Immediately before the festival begins there is a period of fasting. Now as in the old days, this at least is a theory is accompanied by abstinence from sexual intercourse, Then there is the preparation of paximadia, bread rolls and cakes of phallic shape which are made by all village housewives so that they may be eaten over Easter. Such cakes appear frequently in pre-Christian Cypriot ritual. They are mentioned in certain places as offerings to Adonis and Aphrodite, being broken up into small pieces and placed in containers round statues of Adonis.

Special wedding cakes were eaten by the bride and groom at marriage ceremonies and many of the nature spirits associated with Aphrodite were offered similar cakes made of flour, oil and honey. The phallic cakes prepared by modern Cypriot housewives are not all consumed by members of the family. Some of them are given to domestic animals and on the night of 5 January, specially made cakes dipped in honey, are thrown onto the roofs of the houses to be consumed by a fantastic breed of hideous but friendly spirits known as the **Kalikantzari.**

On Good Friday, young women collect aromatic flowers with which they decorate their church and use what is left to make a pile for the funeral bier representing the body of Jesus. On the floor of the church they scatter branches of the Myrtle tree. In the evening of the same day, the bier with its load of flowers is carried through the streets in procession so that the faithful may bid farewell to their dead God. This terminates at the church where it started and the flowers are distributed by the priest among the congregation. On the following day there is another church service, ending at midnight when the resurrection of Christ is proclaimed by the priest. The joyous message is given in the phrase *"Christ is Risen"* and at its utterance, the people light candles, wish happiness to each other, ring church bells, explode fireworks . . . After these ceremonies people return home and as soon as they arrive they greet the plants in their gardens with the phrase *"Christ is Risen, plant"* thus informing them of the arrival of spring. Then they commence preparations for the Easter feast. Men usually kill animals and skin them; the women chop the meat up and cook it. By the morning the atmosphere is filled with the aroma of roasted meat and wood fires.

All monasteries in Cyprus celebrate one or more feasts in honour of a saint or of a holy relic to which they are dedicated. The monastery of Stavrovouni, for instance, is dedicated to the *Holy Cross* and it is there, on 18 September, that a feast is held which attracts pilgrims from many parts of Cyprus. It is an occasion for devotion and merrymaking, not unlike festivals held on the same site in pagan times. After the church service people split into family or village groups and have picnics in the monastery grounds. Occasionally they witness the miraculous cure of a blind person or a cripple, achieved by the most valuable possession of the monastery, a cross which incorporates a small piece of the True Cross given to Stavrovouni by St Helena. The monks of Stavrovouni produce ikons which can be offered to a church or taken home as souvenirs.

The monastery of Stavrovouni is on the summit of a conical mountain and is perched precariously on the mountain's summit. In ancient times and for a thousand years before the birth of Jesus, the temple of *Aphrodite Akrea,* stood on the same spot and here the Cypriots went to pray for rain. The story of Stavrovouni is worth relating because the functions and character of the two religious institutions which have shared it resemble each other to a remarkable degree.

After a long drought that lasted for ten years and almost depopulated the island, St Helena arrived in Cyprus carrying with her the Cross of Christ which she found in Jerusalem. Soon after her arrival the rain began to fall bringing new life to the land. The river at the bottom of Stavrovouni began to flow again and the grateful people renamed it the Queen's River, for Helena was the queen mother of Byzantium. One night Helena slept by the riverside and when she woke in the morning she found to her great distress that the Holy Cross had disappeared from her tent. After a long search it was found on the mountain of Aphrodite where the goddess of love had her temple, so St Helena took it as a sign that she should build a monastery there. This she did and deposited in it part of the true cross renaming the mountain **Stavrovouni** *(The Mount of the Holy Cross).* Over the years countless miracles of healing and rainmaking have been 'performed' by the monks with the assistance of the cross.

Legend has it that Stavrovouni was built using forced labour of a horde of devils, a myth readily accepted by anyone who is acquainted with the topography of the place. Certainly it would have needed pretty devilish work to have approached such as awkward site. Apparently Helena conscripted 40 demons as masons, and when their work was finished she enticed them down a deep well, ostensibly for the purpose of fetching water. However when they were all in she took the opportunity of sealing up the well. The ruins of the pagan temple are still visible at the south-east corner of the monastery.

South West of Stavrovouni, on a hill between the villages of Aplanta and Kivisili there exists a strange shrine dedicated to **St Black,** *(Ayia Mavri)* a lay saint. In common with Aphrodite's companions Delight,

Fulfilment and others, St Black has no distinct personality and she probably derived her name from the black stones which abound around her cave. This saint is another miracle worker specialising in procreative effects and cures for ailments of the stomach. Those who wish to enlist her assistance must offer to her a strip torn from their clothing. The bushes around the shrine are covered with colourful pieces of cloth hanging from their branches. There are other sacred caves, some of which are associated with springs and wells. One is the tomb of **St Barnabas** in Famagusta. Its entrance is shadowed by eucalyptus trees and inside an underground chamber is a well of holy water. The remains of the saint and his bible were removed to Constantinople in the fifth century, but pilgrims from all over the island still visit the tomb to fetch holy water for their sick. As we know holy wells have existed in many countries including Cyprus, from early antiquity and the belief in their medicinal properties is based on the fact that they contain minerals. The monasteries and churches who own these wells have grown rich on the donations of sick people who have been cured.

The worship of saints is not approved of by a new educated church hierarchy in Cyprus but at the village level priests and their parishioners believe in specialised spirits, who are divine and who can help them in specific situations. Thus **St Therapon** is appealed to in case of stomach ache, **St Myriakos** for any pain on the head and **St Anna** to ease the pains of childbirth. There are also saints who protect sailors, drivers, riders, etc., and Our Lady of the Ports protects all travellers who visit her church in Kato Paphos and ask for her assistance. **St Mnason**, the Cypriot saint mentioned in the New Testament, is the protector of people who cheat on a small scale for a good cause. St Paul would have been quite horrified by some of these practices but some church leaders justify them on the grounds that the saints have the power to intercede with God. Saints are bribed in exactly the same way as Aphrodite was in order to gain their favours. The churches of miracle-working saints are extravagantly decorated with presents of gold and silver ornaments given to saints for their services.

The sanctity of relics, familiar to votaries of Aphrodite, is still upheld by Cypriots who believe in the magical properties of the remains of saints and any object associated with them.

Adonis and Aphrodite as a couple had exercised a powerful influence on the imagination of the ancient Cypriots and it is not difficult to find parallels between these two figures and those of Jesus and the Virgin. Of course Jesus is a more important divinity than **Mary** while Aphrodite was superior to Adonis but there are many similarities. As in the case of Aphrodite, Mary's festivals, legends and emblems vary greatly from one place of worship to another, so that to a stranger it might seem that many different divinities are being worshipped rather than one.

Mary's epithets are as numerous as those of Aphrodite: *Madonna of Kykkou, Chrysopolitissa, Sotera* etc. and the title *Queen of Heaven* is shared by both. Jesus and Adonis died violently and were resurrected, and both are incarnate in the instrument of their death. The cross is venerated by Cypriot Christians as deeply as the swine by the votaries of Adonis. Indeed the Christian church has set a special date, 18 September, for the adoration of the cross. Moreover, Jesus, like Adonis, is sacrificed to himself and fed to his worshippers in the mystery of the Holy Communion.

The attitude of Cypriot villagers toward religion in general and to the priesthood in particular is the same as that of their ancestors. It is important to them that the correct forms of worship are kept and they are enthusiastic churchgoers but questions of morality and personal behaviour are divorced from religion. They do not see anything wrong in a church going shopkeeper cheating his customers, or for a religious man (not a woman) to have extra marital affairs if they can get away with it. These are matters for the law or the individual's conscience and not for the church. Priests are not consulted on any social issue except by their nearest relatives and they are not expected to be more knowledgeable, more devout or on a higher moral plane than an average citizen. Their main qualification for their position is an ability to conduct the liturgy efficiently, to perform the rites correctly and to have a good voice for changing the psalms. An interesting aspect of this attitude which denies priests a superior position in society is that meeting a priest unexpectedly is thought to be a bad omen by superstitious Cypriots. Should they see a priest first thing in the morning or to meet one unexpectantly on the way to work, they believe he will bring them bad luck, especially if the priest rides a donkey. To protect themselves they hasten to touch their genitals which are believed to have the kind of magical powers to combat the evil eye, like the phallic god Priapus, the son of Aphrodite, had in ancint times. A little folk rhyme relating to this superstition goes like this:

> '*Should you see a priest pass,*
> *Hold on to your balls fast*'.

Above: Stavrovouni Monastery where once stood a Temple dedicated to Aphrodite.
Below: Spring flower festival, a continuation of the ancient Adonia festivals.

Appendix

Cyprus Through the Years

(See S. Panteli – New History of Cyprus. Pages 415-417)

c.8000—3000BC	Neolithic (or new Stone) Age
c.3000—2500BC	Calcolithic Age
c.2500—2000BC	Early Bronze Age
c.2000—1500BC	Middle Bronze Age
c.1500—1050BC	Late Bronze Age: Settlement of Mycenaean Greeks
1050—58BC	Early Iron Age: Settlement of Phoenicians

8th—5th centuries BC — The established city kingdoms stood up well to the invasions and rule of some of the rising great empires — Assyrians, Egyptians and Persians.

332—323BC — Alexander the Great freed the island and its kings retained their sovereignty. A power struggle between Alexander's successors, Antigonus and Ptolemy, followed for nearly 30 years.

294—58BC — The Ptolemaic Period. Administrative unity was established by means of quasi-military control. The governor had the title of 'strategos' (general) of the island. He was both the civil administrator and the chief of the armed forces.

Paphos becomes an important Ptolemaic centre and the Temple of Aphrodite gets a new lease of life.

The petty kingdoms were abolished. Generally speaking, the relatively peaceful conditions of the island during the greater part of Ptolemaic rule resulted in an expanding population and prosperity.

58BC—AD330 — The Roman Period. Of special importance were the introduction of Christianity in AD45-6 and the massive Jewish rebellion of AD115-6.

Paphos becomes the capital of Roman Cyprus and Aphrodites Temple at Paleapaphos became a centre of Aphrodite's worshipping in the Empire. The Temple is destroyed in 15BC by an earthquake. Rebuilt by Emperor Augustus.

330—1191 — Cyprus became part of the Byzantine Empire.

The period was above all characterized by the autocephaly of the Cypriot Orthodox Church, the Arab raids between the 7th and 10th centuries and the destructive earthquakes of 332 and 342.

The worshipping of Aphrodite was outlawed in Cyprus by Emperor Theodosios in 391AD.

1191   Cyprus came into the hands of Richard I ("Coeur-de-Lion"), King of England. He sold the island to the Order of the Knights Templar.

1192—1489   The Lusignan period.

Economically, socially, politically and culturally, Cyprus was horizontally divided into two separate and distinct sections. At the apex was the feudal class, mostly of French origin, and the foreign merchants, the vast majority being Italian, who resided in the island; at the bottom were the local Greek inhabitants who were mostly serfs and labourers.

The ruling class belonged to the Catholic Church and the Greeks to the Orthodox Church.

The ruling élite spoke mostly French and the masses spoke Greek.

The part played by the Lusignans in building up the civilization of Cyprus was negligible. From 1374 to 1464 Famagusta was ruled by the Genoese Republic.

1489—1571   The Venetian occupation.

Most of the people remained serfs to the nobles and devoid of any rights whatsoever. Venice drew considerable tribute from the island and therefore conditions deteriorated rapidly.

The period was marked by total disinterestedness on the part of the rulers.

1571—1878   The Ottoman occupation.

Cyprus had been made into an eyalet or beglerbegilik, with Muzaffar Pasha as the first governor.

A major contribution towards the welfare of the native Greek population was the Ottoman decision to abolish the Roman Catholic hierarchy and to restore the Orthodox Church of Cyprus under its archbishop. This prelate was made representative of his community *vis-à-vis* the Ottoman government as the ethnarch or head of the Greek community. Turkish rule was marked by growing decay and impoverishment. Trade dwindled, productivity decreased and the population showed a marked decline.

Revolts by both groups of the population occurred at regular intervals. Those of 1680-87, 1745, 1764-6 and

1833 were of particular importance. These risings were put down by force of arms.

The Temple at Paleapaphos suffered extensive damages and destruction by the so-called archaeologist, American, Palma Luigi de Cesnola.

1878—1960   The British occupation.

At a time of extreme fear for its own security and existence, Turkey ceded Cyprus to Britain in 1878. In 1914 the island was annexed and after all rights and claims to the island were renounced by Turkey in 1923, Cyprus became a Crown Colony in 1925. The 'key' to the continents of Europe, Asia and Africa remained a British possession for 82 years. Despite the many difficulties faced by the new administration, the island proved a strategic, political, economic and commercial gain.

Of the many problems which Britain had to face, perhaps the most perplexing was the agitation by the Greek inhabitants for the union of Cyprus with Greece. The Hellenic ideal was much older than the British occupation. Modern Panhellenism silently grew under centuries of foreign domination.

1960—   The Cyprus Republic.

The Zürich-London Agreements of February 1959 finally set up the Cyprus Republic — the 99th member state of the United Nations.

In 1974 Turkey invaded and occupied the northern part of Cyprus which is still inaccessible to citizens of the Republic and its guests.

The Temple of Apollo-Courion where another cult into the worshipping of Apollo Hylates lasted for over 1000 years.

125

Two pictures showing Leda and the Swan – Above: A sculpture by Ammannati – Below: a mosaic found in Paphos (now Cyprus Museum) Zeus is disguised as a swan trying to seduce Leda.

BIBLIOGRAPHY

Casson, L.	*Travel in the Ancient World,* 1974
Casson, S.	*Ancient Cyprus. Its Art and Archaeology,* 1937
Cesnola, L.P. Di	*Cyprus: Its Ancient Cities, Tombs and Temples,* 1877
Clark, K.M.	*The Nude. A Study of Ideal Art,* 1956
Ferguson, J.	*The Religion of the Roman Empire,* 1970
Frazer, J.G.	*The Golden Bough.* 2 Volumes, 1957
Grigson, G.	*The Goddess of Love,* 1976
Guerber, H.A.	*Greece and Rome. Myths and Legends,* 1986
Hadjicostis, G.	*Ktima and New Paphos,* 1970
Hill, G.H.	*History of Cyprus.* 4 Volumes, 1940-1952
Homer	*The Illiad* (Trans. E.V. Rieu — 1953)
James, E.O.	*The Cult of the Mother Goddess,* 1959
James, E.O.	*The Ancient Gods,* 1960
Lavithis, R.G.	*Paphos: Land of Aphrodite,* 1987
Lawson, J.C.	*Modern Greek Folklore and Ancient Religion,* 1910
Lindsay, J.	*The Ancient World: Manners and Morals,* 1968
Luke, H.	*Cyprus: A portrait and an appreciation,* 1965
Morton, H.C.V.	*In the Steps of St. Paul,* 1937
Panteli, S.	*A New History of Cyprus,* 1984
Pinsent, J.	*Myths and Legends of Ancient Greece,* 1969
Wind, E.	*Pagan Mysteries in the Renaissance,* 1967

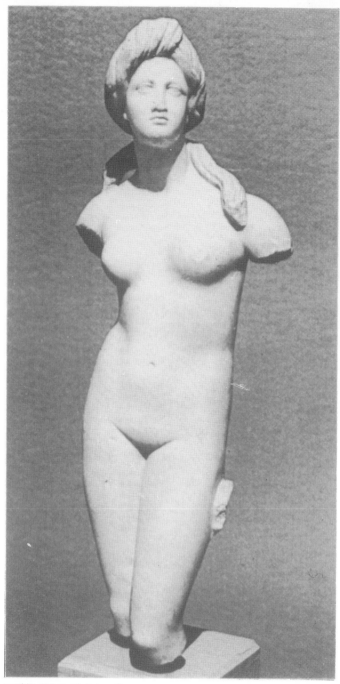

marble statue of Aphrodite
Cyprus Museum.